WHEN LOVING YOUR KID IS A CRIME:

Parents of **TRANSGENDER CHILDREN** Speak Out

RIKI WILCHINS
WITH CLARE HOWELL

For more information contact:
Riverdale Avenue Books
5676 Riverdale Avenue
Riverdale, NY 10471
www.riverdaleavebooks.com

Design by www.formatting4U.com
Cover by Scott Carpenter.

Digital ISBN: 9781626016637
Print ISBN: 9781626016644

First edition, September 2023

ACKNOWLEDGMENTS

Thanks to therapist Jennifer Butzen, who was kind enough to reply to an email from me out-of-the-blue. She helped me get started with my first contacts with parents, and my first interviews for this book.

Your dedication to transchildren and their families is an inspiration.

DEDICATION

To Gina & Dylan: You are my life.

And to Leelah Alcorn
Rest in peace—
Yes, your death did "mean something."

Leelah Alcorn (November 15, 1997 – December 28, 2014) came out at 14. Her conservative Christian parents refused to accept her and at 16, denied her transition care, instead removing her from school, cutting off communication with her friends, and forcing her into a Christian-based conversion therapy program. According to Leelah they would also say things like, "You'll never be a real girl; "What're you going to do, fuck boys?" and "God's going to send you straight to hell."

In 2014 Leelah put a suicide note on her Tumblr account to be posted automatically that ended up appearing after her death that that read in part:"

"I'm never going to be happy. Either I live the rest of my life as a lonely man who wishes he were a woman or I live my life as a lonelier woman who hates herself. There's no winning. There's no way out. I'm sad enough already, I don't need my life to get any worse. People say 'it gets better' but that isn't true in my case. It gets worse. Each day I get worse....

Three days after Christmas, 2014, Leelah walked out onto I-71 not far from her Kings Mills, Ohio home and into the path of an oncoming tractor trailer. She was killed instantly. Her Tumblr note had ended with the words: "My death needs to mean something. My death needs to be counted in the number of transgender people who commit suicide this year. I want someone to look at that number and say 'that's fucked up' and fix it. Fix society. Please."

TABLE OF CONTENTS

"Greg was talking to a friend who was sharing their fun high school memories and he just looked at them: 'My high school memories are testifying at the Capitol. That's all I know. When people ask me about high school, I tell them I spent my entire high school career running up to the Capitol testifying for my life."

So no prom, no dances, none of that stuff. Greg's main high school memory was, "Please don't pass this law and kill me."

"It took me four days to drive to Connecticut with three kids, four cats and three lizards (bearded dragons). We lived out of our van. If we had to go to the bathroom, I drive to the gas station. For food, we've been living meal to meal.

At night, I park at a truck stop on the Interstate where there's someone on duty 24/7 and the kids just curl up in their seats to sleep. It's getting cold now, so I have to run the engine every now and then to keep us warm at night. But being here is still better than being back there."

CHAPTER 3 – Kaylee

"If it had not been for Chloe, I could have been one of those people attacking the Capitol on January 6th. That's how my family is. I was an ordained minister at the time, and I spent the better part of a year making Chloe's life horrible doing what I thought was right. Chloe was only three or four, but everyone thought the devil was trying to use her for evil. After a year of conversion therapy, she was praying to go to heaven and be with Jesus, so she could be a girl. She would rather go to heaven and be with Jesus and live as herself for eternity, than stay here and live as boy one more day."

CHAPTER 4 – Juno

"I was always in an abusive relationship, but it took my daughter coming out for me to realize how badly abusive it was. My husband has a lot of guns. He loves his guns. And if there's a domestic assault, he knew they'll take your guns. So after that, I wasn't really worried about anything physical, because his guns mean more to him than anything, He wanted me to choose between him and the kids. Well, I chose our kids."

CHAPTER 5 – Kay

"We were on Main Street in the busiest part of downtown. And she's in tears. My whole world stopped and cracked open. I crouched down, wrapped her in my arms, and kept saying, "I love you, it's going to be okay." I felt this weight lift off her shoulders. It was as if in that instant, she stepped into a new skin."

PREFACE
The War on TransYouth

In 1995 when we launched the Gender Public Advocacy Coalition or "GenderPAC" as the first national trans political advocacy organization, it was roundly ignored. We couldn't buy any mention in the media, and even the anti-gay right didn't bother attacking us.

Transpeople—which back then mostly meant adult transsexual women—were considered too small and bizarre a fringe group to bother with. Politically we were less than irrelevant. We were even part of the LGB-but-not-T rights movement.

About the only time transgender rights received any political attention or GenderPAC got any press was when some city or corporation somewhere allowed a transsexual woman (and it was *always* a woman) to use the Women's Room. Then the heavens fell. As far as the public knew, we might as well have been named the Gender Public Bathroom Coalition.

But barely more than two decades later—in the wake of three successful Supreme Court decisions invalidating anti-sodomy laws, banning anti-gay discrimination, and legalizing gay marriage—an enraged and vengeful evangelical Christian right began casting about any issue to reignite its stalled war on homosexuality and launch a new social panic.

And the elephant in that room would be transgender people, who had become the biggest Achilles heel of what was now the "LGBT" movement. The public may have largely accepted gays and lesbians, but its discomfort with transgender people was real and widespread, even among the left, and especially among white

i

evangelical Christians who were virtually the only major demographic that was till staunchly and virulently anti-gay.

In 2018 young people in all 50 states still freely got hormones and medical care, legally changed their names and pronouns, and played gender-appropriate school sports without anyone seeming to care, even across red states, We couldn't know it then, but it was a false dawn, and behind it would come terror.

The evangelical Christian right had been quietly investing millions surveying our political weaknesses, creating focus-grouped messaging, crafting model laws, and creating legitimate-sounding but fake medical front groups. And beginning in 2019 they struck back with a vengeance. In just a few years, more than 1,000 bills would be introduced across more than half of the United States, the vast majority targeting transgender kids.

Being virulently anti-trans was transformed overnight from a minor local issue to a national litmus test, a core element of MAGA tribal identity. The two leading Republican candidates for the Presidency both released simultaneous statements attacking transgender youth for *hacking off body parts, mutilation,* or *left-wing gender insanity.*

The genders of a few thousand children were now a defining issue in the 2024 presidential stakes and, by extension, the fate of the country.

Adult transsexual women like me, who had always been the more socially visible and least politically digestible, had always been the targets of any political vitriol. But suddenly transgender kids and the parents who loved them had become the bleeding edge of transgender rights, and indeed of the entire LGBTQ+ rights movement. It became illegal in a dozen states to provide your child any recommended gender affirming care, including psychotherapy. In states like Texas, allowing your child hormones, blockers, or "top surgery" became felony child abuse, punishable with imprisonment and the lose of your child into the state's byzantine, Christian-based childcare system.

Parents began fleeing their home states in fear, creating a

new class of thousands of displaced internal political refugees in the U.S.—a phenomenon perhaps unknown since the terrible pre-Civil War days of chattel slavery.

It was a turning of history. The decades the "soft transphobia" of ignoring transpeople were gone and had closed behind us forever. From now on, the evangelical Christian right would level all the fury it had devoted to demonizing homosexuality going back to the Lavender Scare of the 1950s at transgender people.

The War on Trans Youth had begun in earnest. It would come to define transgender rights, and—like the battles over sodomy, gay marriage, or gays in the military—it would consume the next 20 years

I began reaching out and interviewing as many gender affirming parents as I could. Many were understandably wary and many demurred. I immediately noticed a stark difference between blue and red state parents. The former had children who came out, transitioned, and got medically-recommended medical care without problem. While they may have endured some transient mispronouning or taunting, their friends, families, and schools were largely supportive and their lives went on as before.

Meanwhile across red states, the parents I spoke with were living in fear, with many in the midst of leaving behind careers, pensions, dream homes, and extended family forever, simply because they loved their children. Some were living out of cars and sleeping at night on the interstate; others were the subject of multiple concurrent investigations by their states; and still others were so scared they are in the process of taking their children out of the country until they were 18. These interviews became the focus of this book.

After every interview, I thanked parents for their courage in standing up for their child, explaining that if I had had just *one* parent like them, my body would be totally different today, my entire *life* would be totally different. Loving your child is no easy thing when it costs you everything. To me, they are American heroes.

But this is where the evangelical Christian rights' War on Trans Youth has taken us .

It is a war we must win.

Our children are depending on us.

Riki Wilchins
2023

**[*You can follow my regular writing on trans and gender politics at Medium.com/RikiWilchins]*

CHAPTER 1: LINDA

PARENT: Linda
Sexual Orientation: Straight
Gender Identity: Female
Age: 38

CHILD: Greg
Gender Identity: Trans Male
Pronouns: He/him
Sexual Orientation: Queer
Age: 18

> *"Greg was talking to a friend who was sharing their fun high school memories. Greg just looked at them and said, 'My high school memories are testifying at the Capitol. That's all I know. When people ask me about high school, I tell them I spent my entire high school career running up to the Capitol testifying for my life."*
> *So no prom, no dances, none of that stuff. Greg's main high school memory was, "Please don't pass this law and kill me."*

What about moving to some sort of states that are safe for trans. But they're all so expensive. And eventually we settled on New Zealand. I don't think it'll ever be safe enough to come back to the States. Greg said something as he was walking away—"Well, it doesn't matter, because I'm never coming back, because they want me dead." He's my only child. Am I really going to ask him to come back to visit me in a state that wants him dead?

1

We first realized that something was different about Greg's gender probably when he was four or five, maybe even earlier. He refused to wear dresses at 18-months-old. And I remember specifically that his biological father, my ex-husband, had come home from Iraq, and we were going to some special military honor dinner. My ex had bought Greg a dress and he was standing at the top of the stairs and threw the dress down at us and screamed, "Boys don't wear dresses." And I was like, "That's correct. But you're not a boy." I was able to get him dressed, but not in a dress—in a pair of pants and a shirt.

I'm a stay-at-home mom. We used to have playgroups at the park and grocery shopping. We'd hang out at friends' houses with kids. I'd have to get him to the pediatrician, or we'd go to the grocery store. So to me the question was, Can I get him dressed and do the things I need to do, before we have playgroup? Eventually I'd just tell him, Okay, you want to wear a dress? My grandma in Alabama used to say, Don't make a mountain out of a molehill. So if you don't want to wear a dress, what do you want to wear? And as long as he was wearing clothes and I could get him out of the house dressed in something, I considered it a win.

Greg was very independent from birth. He always knew what he wanted. I couldn't get him to wear shoes until he was four because he hated them. He did not like us doing his hair at all. I've always had short hair, so I kept his kind of short when he was little. He had dark brown hair, like mine when he was born. It all fell out at two months old and came back in white blonde. So he looked bald until he was probably two, two-and-a-half. He had hair, but it was thin, wispy white hair. People always mistook him for a boy, which is why I think when he was a baby, I made him wear pink and dresses before he had an opinion so that people would remark, Oh, she's so cute; but, because he was bald, people say, Oh, he's so cute. And I'm telling them, She's in a flippin' dress, you know. But I guess they were right.

Once he got a little older and his hair got a little cute and curly, he didn't like me washing it. He didn't like me brushing it.

2

When he was 11 or so, he wanted to grow it out long because his stepmom had long hair. He wouldn't brush it himself. He didn't want to put it up. He didn't want to do anything with it. So I would have to detangle it and brush it and he would scream and cry and throw a tantrum. It would be like we were murdering somebody. From ages three to 11 I kept it pretty short, like shoulder length or shorter, because it was such a pain. And the longer it got, the nastier it got. If you ever had to pull knots out of a kid's hair, it's not fun. I have this T-shirt my mom bought him for Christmas one year. It says Messy Hair, Don't Care. That was just Greg. He didn't want to brush his hair to go to school the next day. No, I'll just go with this crazy rat's nest.

Greg's biological dad was really mad about his refusing to wear dresses. He wanted a girly girl. If you've ever met a toddler, you know they can be awful. It was a big win just to get Greg out of the house wearing clothes at all. He's not going to wear dresses, fine. I was always a tomboy. I still consider myself a tomboy. I'm a jeans and a T-shirt kind of girl, so to me it wasn't surprising. I was like, Cool, let's put clothes on and go to the park or do whatever we have to do for the day. Once he started expressing a preference, I didn't make a big deal out of it, and I never forced him to wear dresses. You don't want to wear dresses? No big deal. So we stopped buying them.

At four or five, I bought him Barbies and he sacrificed the Barbies for G.I. Joes. I tried to get him to play with Barbies because I used to love to play Barbies. He didn't want to. The couple I gave him, he beheaded. She was a victim. He had his GI Joes and then it was Legos. After that he wanted a blue scooter, so we got him one. His first bike at eight years old was a bright orange BMX bike. I chalked it up to more tomboy behavior.

Probably around age eight or nine people started asking me if I thought he was gay. I told them he was just a kid and I didn't care. It just wasn't a discussion I was going to have. But one thing he tells me that he remembers me doing is he loved the board game, Life. So on occasions when we played Life, I would marry a girl and I would tell him, Okay, you can marry a girl. If you're a girl, you can marry a boy. If you're a boy, it doesn't matter who you love. I was trying to open it up for him, in case he wanted to say something. But usually all I got back from him was, "Would you just spin again and, like, shut up." But he always knew that if he was gay, it would be okay for him to come and tell me.

He was 11 when he told me he was a lesbian. He sent me a text when I was at work and he was on his way to school and I answered right away: "Cool, well, you know, have a good day at school. Don't forget to empty the dishwasher when you get home and we'll talk if you want." When I got home and he was like, "That's it?"

I had an inkling, so I said, "I'm glad you're comfortable and that you're figuring out who you are, that's great. I support you no matter what and like I've always told you, I love you no matter what." He did the lesbian thing for almost two years, and then a week before his 13th birthday, he came and told me he was trans, that he was my son.

I honestly had considered myself a good ally, but I don't know anything about the trans community. He told me, I understand if you don't love me. I understand if you want me to go with my dad instead. I understand if you never want to see me again. What is this conversation about? But I told him I loved him no matter what, and that I would always be there for him. But I needed to do a little research. Then he said, "Well, I got homework to do. I'm going to go take a shower. And he walked off.

I immediately Googled, "What are you supposed to say when your kid tells you he's trans, so you don't screw him up for life?" I had reassured him that I loved him and that he was always going to be welcome with me. I knew what the trans terminology was, but I didn't know anyone in the community. I didn't know what to do. Over the next weeks I did even more Googling. Greg knows I'm a big science nerd so he came to me with PowerPoints and Excel spreadsheets about starting puberty blockers, starting T, getting top surgery. He already had it figured out. I told him,

"Time out. It hasn't been three minutes. I don't know what's happening. I'm sure we'll get there eventually, but I'm glad you found all these facts." And some of it was really helpful to me. But he was insistent, "Let's start puberty blockers today." I didn't even know how we would do that. Where do we start? I Googled some more. I found our state Equality group, and reached out to them: "Help, I don't know what to do." They connected me with TENT, the state trans organization, who then connected me with some parents of trans kids who I'm still friends with.

But I still have many of the same questions: Where do I go? What do I do? And how do I tell people? There are Facebook groups around these issues, but they're all private and would have to invite me in. It was February—the end of Greg's seventh grade year—so we went with the philosophy of Let's just finish up this year. We immediately got a haircut, changed his clothes, so he was presenting very masculine, but still going by like his deadname. We weren't changing all that, because school was almost over and we were still trying to figure it out. That was also 2017, when the bathroom bill stuff was still going on, and we were waiting to see because we didn't know if he'd have any rights at school if he transitioned socially.

So he finished seventh grade year and then we let him complete the social transition. We were trying to find names and I told him, I get the mom veto, because I would have chosen a name for you if you had been born male. You don't get a say. We'll try out names for a week. Then if one of us doesn't like it, either one can veto it. He tried out Marcus. I don't know why, but I hated it. It just wasn't him and I vetoed that. I really liked Ethan, which he had previously liked until he knew I liked it, and he vetoed it after two days. But then a friend of a friend had just had a baby named Greg and she had suggested we try it. I gave it to him, and he was into trying it out, and after a week we both said, That's it. This fits.

Pronouns were a little harder. I was used to the female pronouns, so I kept messing up, and it was making him angry.

We had been able to find a good psychologist for him. Because Greg was getting very angry with me and acting out, the psychologist suggested, "Get a spray bottle, spray your mom. That way you're not slamming doors and screaming at her." So he sprayed me whenever I misgendered him and after he hit me with that a few times, I stopped pretty quickly. I wore glasses, and him being a little jerky 13-year-old, he would get me right in the face, spray the glasses, so he would make sure it counted. With the help of our state transgender and Equality group, we were able to find a psychologist in the area and a doctor. I still wasn't doing things fast enough for Greg, because he told me that we should have had puberty blockers the next day. Like everything should have been done yesterday. To him, as fast as I was trying to move, I was still dragging my feet. We still hadn't told the school. I was trying to get all the information I could so that I would be able to best present it to the school, to best protect him and make sure that... to be honest, I didn't know what the hell I was doing. I'm one step at a time, please.

We were able to find a good psychologist. Greg's biological father is military so all three of us had military insurance. It turns out there one doctor on our military base who sees all the trans kids. Fort Hood is one of the largest army bases in the US. So they sent us to this doctor who, to this day, even though we don't have that insurance anymore and we haven't seen him in four years, still emails every so often to check up on us and see how we're doing. Going in, I asked if he was a specialist. He answered that, No, he's just the one who takes the trans kids. He said he didn't start out seeing trans kids. He actually had a family practice in osteopathy. But in 2012 he had a patient who was a trans kid, and he went and educated himself. Then suddenly all his patients were trans, because nobody else on the base wanted to deal with it. So he took them. Greg has chronic health issues, so he was dealing with that too, on top of the trans stuff.

That doc was amazing, a lifesaver. I feel like they should have had more than one doctor for trans kids in such a large army base. But he saw us pretty quickly, and when we met with him he said, All right, here's how we're going to get puberty blockers, if that's what we want to do. I knew my ex-husband wasn't going to be on-board with that. He was a tank mechanic. We got divorced in 2011, and I think he got out of the service in 2013. He did three tours in Iraq, and one in Afghanistan. He'd had inklings that Greg was more than just the tomboy we thought, and he'd always say that if Greg was gay or trans, he wasn't going to put up with it.

We were able to talk to Greg's counselor and his doctor about the pros and cons and they gave us lots of articles. I'm very scientific minded. Show me the data. I wanted to have all that in hand when we told his biological father who was remarried by this time to his second wife. I believe he's on the way for three or four now. But I called his second wife and was explaining that we had something we wanted to FaceTime them about, to give her a heads-up that something was coming. And right away she asked me, Is it a gender thing? And I said Yeah, because she wanted to prep my ex because she knew it was not going to go well.

We called on my cell phone and did a FaceTime. When Greg told him, dad threw the iPad and stormed out. I had already sent all the information to his current wife at the time so they could review it. He didn't talk to me or Greg for three to five days. He finally sent Greg an apology text, Sorry. I got mad. It's all just so new to me.

He kept telling me, "No medical interventions. It's fine that he's seeing a psychologist, it's fine that you're calling him this name and using male pronouns." I think that was mostly his wife's doing, getting him to agree to the social aspects. But he was adamant that absolutely nothing medical happen until Greg was 18. I hadn't gotten that far in my research on surgeries, but I understood puberty blockers and the effect a big chest would have on him. I was thinking, No offense, but everyone in my family is D boobs or bigger. He's 13. We're going to traumatize him a thousand times worse. Greg already was developing a chest, and I told my ex that he really didn't like that or how he was having periods.

We agreed on blocker shots that helped stop breast growth, because it was just so dysphoric and horrible for our son to deal with. And thankfully they worked. But it seemed like every day Greg was asking me, Is my chest bigger? I feel like it's bigger. I found out he was wearing two or three sports bras backwards because we didn't have a binder, which he wanted. I told him I wanted to do more research on binders.

I remember one of our psychologists calling me in and sitting me down and saying, I understand you like to have all the information. But your son is hurting himself. He's wearing sports bras that are too small and backward. I'm telling you, he can't do it overnight. I'm telling you, these are the best ways to do it. But if you don't buy him a binder, he's going to continue hurting himself.

So I actually called my mom because I told my parents that he was trans and I didn't know what to do. And she bought him a binder. A 60-something-year-old grandma's on Amazon, buying my son binders. That was amazing to me, because at first my mom was very upset and aggrieved about Greg's transition. And now she asking me, "How many do we need?" I've heard parents say that they grieve the child they thought they were losing. My mom grieved the granddaughter she thought she had. I didn't grieve, because I still got to tuck the same loving kid into bed every night. To me it was, "Oh, now I truly know who he is." So I wasn't grieving, but she still had issues. She was reading Caitlyn Jenner's book. I know she's not the best example, but that book really resonated with my mom.

My mom saw so many things that Greg did as a kid. That was the next conversation after she finished the book. How did we miss all the signs? How did we not know for 13 years? How are we so stupid? Greg was telling us every which way possible and we just missed it. Her favorite story to tell people was when he was five or six years old and staying at her house for the summer. They were playing in the basement with some baby dolls and she said, Oh, you're such a good mommy. And Greg looked at her and he says, "No, I'm a good daddy. Boys can be good daddies, right?" "Yes," she said. And she didn't think anything else of it.

But Greg was always the daddy when he played with friends and we never really paid that much attention to it. My biggest regret is that he had to go 13 years being misgendered, dealing with all that dysphoria and pain. Looking back, I can see it all now, but hindsight's 20/20. When he tried so many different ways: I don't wear dresses. I want to play the dad. I want the orange BMX bike. It wasn't a big deal to me, but I realized it was to him. They were all different ways of him telling me, "Hey, mom, I'm your son." But it all went over my head and that's what I really regret. That it literally took him telling me, I'm trans, to understand that he was my son since he was 18-months-old. I hate that. I just didn't know enough. I didn't know any better.

He had been to a psychologist after his father and I got divorced in 2011, when Greg was seven. And he told them all that stuff too, and they didn't catch it either. So I can't blame myself too much. The doctor tells me not to blame myself. I thought I was doing everything right, and still somehow missed the big neon sign.

Even Greg says, I 100% knew. I always knew I was different. He thought there was something wrong. He said, "I thought it was because I was gay, at first." So he had to figure some of it out. I don't think he blames me. I blame myself more than he ever will, because once he came out, I was 100% on board. But seeing other kids who got to start puberty blockers, who don't have to have top surgery, they won't have all the dysphoria he had. If I could go back to at least eight-year-old Greg, before puberty, and figure it all out, I would do it in a heartbeat, because it would have made his next few years so much better.

I was definitely scared when Greg first told me. I mean, scared. What are other people going to say? One of the first facts I Googled was the murder rate of trans people, which was probably not the best thing to learn your first five minutes into it. But that's the first thing that pops up when you Google the subject. And I had a lot of gay and queer friends and I knew how hard it was for them to just be gay. It is hard for anyone in the LGBTQ+ community, I get that. But being trans seems to be like the most stigmatized identity now.

When I was finally ready to tell everybody, we told immediate family first. How do I have this conversation? My parents were in their 60s; how am I going to tell them? And how are we going to deal with bullies? We knew at the time, well, I don't know if he knew; but, I knew about the legislative session going on with the bathroom bills being about trans folks. I don't even know what to do with school. How do you do any of this? So I was in research mode. I thought about my ex-husband, his dad. I was thinking he was going to lose his shit. And my next thought was, he's going to blame it on me and I really don't care. Maybe he'll just leave us alone, totally cut us off, and we'll be good. I won't have to deal with him anymore.

I made the big Facebook announcement, "This is my son. So if you hear me referring to my son by this name now, you know. It's the same child that I've been talking about for the last 13 years." Ninety percent of the comments I got back were along the lines of: It's about time you figured it out. I am not shocked at all. Woo hoo! So glad he finally figured it out. I thought: If y'all knew, why didn't anyone point it out to me? How did everyone else but me know, anyhow? But a lot of them were like this, "Well, once you said it, it was, Oh, that makes sense." But until it was specifically said, it didn't click for them either. I feel stupid about that too, because we've since met so many families in our community whose kids transitioned at age four or five. How awesome would that have been for him?

So after the end of seventh grade, when we were still using

his female pronouns and birth name, school was finally over in May. During that summer before his eighth grade, I reached out to his school and let them know his name was Greg and that he was trans. I had a bunch of information I had gotten online to give them. I thought, I can educate them. And their response was, "We need to send a letter out to all the parents and let them know a trans student will be coming to school." I told them, "Absolutely not. Hold on. You're not outing him to the whole world." What were they thinking? That he might be contagious or something?

Ninety percent of the kids were amazing when he came into eighth grade, Hey, I'm Greg. They were like, Oh, that makes sense. Most of his friends were cool with it, because he was already in short hair and masculine clothes at the end of seventh grade. I met with the school a couple of times over the summer, still trying to educate them. They agreed not to send out the letter to everyone. Fine, they said, we'll call him whatever name or pronouns you want, but he still has to use the girls' bathroom. But Greg wouldn't do that. So he had to use the nurse's bathroom. I believe the bathroom bill had been defeated in July, but I didn't know if schools would enforce it anyway. Greg was fine with the nurse's bathroom, because he was definitely not going to use the girls' bathroom.

As for Phys Ed and using the locker room, we got a doctor's note to get Greg out of gym because they wanted him in the girls' locker room. We weren't doing that. And he does have chronic health issues. So his doctor was willing to write him a note saying that he couldn't do gym. So he sat on the bleachers and watched his class do stuff, because he wasn't going to change in the girls' locker room.

I met with all of his eighth grade teachers. I emailed each of them because the school basically told me to figure out how to tell people before Meet the Teacher Night. I told them that if they wanted any information to let me know and some of them emailed back asking for resources. And not a single teacher on Meet the Teacher Night dead-named him or used female pronouns. They all knew his name and his pronouns and they all greeted him correctly. I was expecting a few flubs, since they had never met him before, but there were none. It was actually pretty impressive.

But the principal, I hated her. She told us she had to use his legal name for school records. Okay, that's fine. But I wanted to make sure that he was called by the correct name and pronouns. To which she said, "Well, if you want to contact the teachers, I can't force them to do any of this—what do you call it—crazy gender goofiness or something." The teachers were already accepting, but the principal was arguing back, telling me that they couldn't just call students whatever name they wanted. I think the principal was irritated because she never wanted anyone like us in her school. But there was really no issue with Greg until he had substitute teachers. The list the subs get has the kids' legal names, and Greg's legal name was different. When they called out his legal name, he would have to correct them and say his pronouns. When the sub would get the wrong name, there were a couple kids who didn't like him and would start dead-naming him and stuff. Since the teacher called you this, I'm going to do it too. Greg would let me know and I'd call the principal or go meet with her and tell her what had happened with the sub. Well, she'd say, they're calling him his real name.

"No," I'd say, "this is bullying," And she'd tell me, "It's on his birth certificate." And I just lost it, "These kids don't frickin' know what's on his birth certificate: they're 13-year-old boys and girls. How can we fix this?" And she tells me, "Well, I guess any time he has a sub, we could cross out his real name and put the name you like." "But why can't you just put it in the system?" And her secretary speaks up, "Oh, we could do it in the system." And the principal overrules her, and says, "No, it has to be the legal name in the system."

Obviously, for state testing, you have to use your legal name, and we were ready for that. But the principal was throwing a fit, saying, "He's turning in paperwork with that name on it."

But his teachers know who he is. They're putting it in the grade book for the right kid. I understand for state standardized testing he has to use his legal name and we're ready for that. But for a spelling test or his English paper, his teachers know who he is. So why can't he just write Greg? Because eighth grade was so horrible and school was so bad for him, he ended up going to high school online and was able to graduate in three years.

We ended up almost suing Greg's school that year to allow him to use the bathrooms and for him to have the correct name. He was using the nurse's bathroom, but it was on the opposite side of the school from where the eighth grade classes were. He used it three or four times, but it's a big school and, because he didn't have enough time to get there and back, he'd ask for a pass for class. The nurse told him, "I'm not giving you passes. You're just doing this to be late." The deal had been for him to use the nurse's bathroom, and then she would give him a note so he didn't get in trouble for being late to class. I didn't find all this out until he had UTIs because he was holding it all day. So after that I told them to let him use a different bathroom. And one of the other parents connected me to an ACLU lawyer who was willing to help us pro bono. We had a group meeting with the school around the bathroom issue and the substitute teachers dead-naming him. His school bus tried to segregate the kids by gender, with boys on one side, girls on the other. Greg went to the boys' side, but some kids were doing some pretty nasty, mean things to him, saying he doesn't belong on either side. When the other kids made fun of him and were dead-naming him and bullying him, the school did nothing. With the ACLU lawyer, eventually they said he could use whatever bathroom he felt most comfortable in. His friends would actually check to make sure the boys' room was empty and then stand protection outside to make sure nothing happened while he used it. The school never did change his name on the roster for the subs, although they agreed to.

I was leaving work two or three days a week to go down and

yell at the principal about a kid bullying him or, calling the school every morning to say, "Does Greg have any subs?"

"Yes?"

"Have you changed the name on the roster for that class?"

"Oh, let me do that now."

I did that every morning to make sure that he wouldn't be dead-named, and they would still mess it up. It was such a hateful environment for a young kid, he just couldn't take it anymore. It got so anxiety-inducing for Greg, he was having panic attacks. He couldn't go to school. So his doctor wrote him off for the last month-and-a-half of eighth grade. I would pick up his schoolwork, he'd do it, and then I'd drop it off every week. Then one day they were handing me his schoolwork and the principal came out, and yanked it out of my hands, telling me, No, he doesn't get to do any work while he's out. He's excused. His grades are frozen right where they are now. We won't change anything. So I made her give that to me in writing because she wouldn't let him do the last month-and-a-half of schoolwork. She did give it to me in writing. His grades were already good, so they stayed that way. He just came and took the Star State test over two days and that was it.

Unfortunately he had to take it in the principal's office. She made everything for my kid 10 times worse than it ever had to be. I found out later she has a gay son, whom she disowned, and now she tells people she has no children. Her maiden was Miss Loving, which I thought was hilarious because she was the least loving person I ever fucking met. I do not like her.

In seventh grade, Greg had dated his friend Kat, who is bisexual. He was identifying as a girl then. But after he came out as trans, they were just friends because she said she didn't like guys. So he didn't really date anyone, although I know he had a crush on his current partner, and they've liked each other since eighth grade. His current partner lives with us. He moved in with us after he graduated high school. They have been in love since they were 13. They're both 18 now. But they weren't really dating. They were just good friends. I don't think he was really looking to date. I told him, "I know you're not dating anyone now, but if you think about dating someone, we're going to have some deep discussions and figure that out." He said, "I just want to go to class, get my puberty blockers, and be done with middle school." Middle school is hard all the time and being the only trans kid in school made it a thousand times worse. Not to mention his principal was a bigot.

Greg started puberty blockers that in 2017 when he was 13, and started hormones two years later in 2019 when he was 15. It was delayed because we had to terminate his biological father's rights before we could start hormones. The doctor had told us that blockers were reversible and he only needed one parent's permission. So I did it behind my ex-husband's back. The custody dispute started in 2018 when he was 14, and we didn't get his dad's rights terminated till 2019. It was a long, nasty custody battle. Greg got top surgery two years ago yesterday, in December of 2020, just before he turned 17.

When he'd first come or told me he was trans, I told him, "No surgeries till you're 18." We wanted top surgery a little early because he'd finished high school early and was going to go off to college and once there, he would be living in the boy's dorm. He didn't want to have to be hiding his chest all the time behind binders and lose clothes. So we knew before he left for college we were going to do top surgery. We found a surgeon that we liked and we were actually able to get on his calendar.

December 8th is my dad's birthday, so he laughed and says that his birthday present was getting rid of Greg's boobs on his 70th birthday. I knew we had picked a good surgeon. He was a local surgeon, so we didn't have to travel. That was important to me, because I know recovery is hard. You don't want to be in a hotel room. People do it, but I felt like he'd be more comfortable at home. I knew it was what was best for Greg. But I was still really nervous, and then I was a nervous wreck during the surgery. Greg was super excited, didn't sleep the night before, couldn't wait. We got there and, because of COVID, they took him back alone. When they finally wheeled him out to me, he was sitting in a wheelchair, still very loopy. But he looked at me with this big smile and said, "Mom, I'm finally free." That's all we needed. That made it all worth it. He tried to stand up and giggled, "Mom, I'm drunk."

He used to shower in the dark, because he didn't like to see his breasts. That was a concession we made in accord with his psychologist. You have to take showers, but you can shower in the dark. For two weeks after surgery we had to give him very gentle sponge baths. But the first time he took a shower after top surgery, I remember walking past the bathroom and I saw the light on. I cried, because he took a shower with the lights on. It had been five years since he had done that. I was ecstatic that it gave him so much more peace of mind. And I was less worried about him going away to college, 1300 miles from us, because now he wouldn't have to be binding and hiding in the boys' bathroom.

After we terminated his biological father's rights, we legally changed his name and his gender marker. So now his college would know him only as a guy. He was going to live in the men's dorm. My big concern before top surgery was an intolerant roommate: What if they catch him binding or something? He's actually good friends with his freshman college roommate now. But with top surgery, he was safer. He didn't have to change in front of his roommate, but if he wanted to, it would be just scars. He used to joke that if anyone said anything, he was going to tell people he'd been attacked by a shark. It brought me peace of mind to know that he didn't have to try to hide what to him was a deformity. He wanted to go around with no shirt on for the first time and, because he didn't go off to college till Fall of 2021, he had four or five months at home finishing up high school and every time he was out in the living room, he had no shirt on. I just let it be. But eventually sometime in February or March it got cold and I told him, "You have to put a shirt on." And he's like,

"No, I don't." To which I said, "I'm not going anywhere with you in this cold without a shirt on."

He went out of state to Indiana University last year, and Indiana is a very red state. Even though he enjoyed his first year, we decided we were going to see about switching schools. There are a lot of safe states. But it made me think of what he said as we were talking about it. He said something like, "Well, it doesn't matter. I'm never coming back because they want me dead."

He's my only child. Even if he wasn't my only child, he's my child. Am I really going to ask him to come back to visit me in a state that wants him dead? So what safe states can we go to? California is expensive, Connecticut's expensive, Massachusetts... they're all so expensive. I made a flippant comment like, "Well, if it's going to cost me an arm and a leg and I'm going to live broke the rest of my life, we might as well go someplace cool like Australia." He looked at me and said, "Why don't we? Well, I guess we could look into like leaving the country." We settled on New Zealand, because they have good, high-ranking colleges. And I'm going for my master's and PhD while he and his partner are going to go for their bachelors.

Amsterdam, the Netherlands, is number one for trans safety. However, I don't speak Dutch, so that was an issue. I feel like if I'm going to move my entire world to a different country, I at least want to speak the language. I know that limits us a lot. But I don't want to be driving down the road in our new country and not know what the signs say. Plus not many countries are handing out work visas to social workers like me. So we both went for student visas, which is the easiest way to get into most countries. How could we attend school in Germany, where a lot of them speak English and which is very friendly but we didn't speak German. I think it's rude to move somewhere and expect everyone else there to speak your language. So Australia and New Zealand have always been at the top of my list of places to move.

It's really hard moving somewhere else, especially another country. It's expensive and scary and confusing and life-changing. I'm leaving a career I've had for the past three years that I absolutely adore. I do not know if I'll find another job I love this much. The dream house I built in 2020 for my husband and Greg is now on the market. Selling my dream house will fund our move. I know that I will probably never be able to buy another house in the US. It's just the way it is. I'm not going to make enough to afford a house in California or Massachusetts or Connecticut. Which is why we decided to make it an adventure and go to New Zealand. At least there I feel like there're national laws in place and great education opportunities for all of us.

I remember telling my ex-husband when we were divorcing that I wanted to leave the country. I want to go travel and take the kid and we're going to go live in Australia for a couple of years but he wouldn't let it happen. He had his lawyer file in court so we couldn't leave the state, even though he had moved to Tennessee. So all my traveling and wanting to move didn't happen, until Greg was 18. Although we ended up terminating his dad's rights when he was 15, here we were still living in a small southern town only a couple states.

So we moved to a blue city and then built a house in the suburbs where we live now. It's safer. Except for the next door neighbors who built their house after us. About a year later, Trump flags are hanging everywhere. They saw my son and his partner holding hands. Called them *faggots* and stuff. So even though the city's blue, not everyone is progressive.

I've called the sheriff on them a couple of times like when they tried to poison our dogs because they were mad at us. They used cigarettes, because nicotine poisoning is a thing. Luckily, only one of the dogs ate them because they taste bad and he threw up a bunch, but he was okay. But the purpose of doing it was to poison the dogs. Our realtor who's selling our house is gay. They scared away our previous realtor by calling him a faggot and throwing shit at him.

We talked to the sheriff again. He said that unless it's videotaped, you don't have proof. Even though three of us saw this happen, he said if they didn't hit us with anything it's not assault. I don't really think it's just harassment. Once we were able to get them a ticket because it was in the summer and they were doing the cigarette thing, we found a lit cigarette. That was a fire hazard and they got a fine. But it was a stupid thing, like you tried to burn down our house because there's a drought. That wasn't what they were trying to do, but it was the only way to get to them.

When Greg says, *The state wants me dead.* It's more than just a general fear. We testified before the state legislature at the 2019 session and the 2021 sessions, and we'll probably do this 2023 session before we get out. So it's not just some neighbors who don't like us, it's probably the legislators too. There was a bill we testified on. It was about should gender identity play a role in custody hearings. His gender identity was extremely important in my custody hearing.

We wanted to testify on that because the bill was going to make it so you couldn't bring up the child's gender identity in a custody hearing. A parent denying their child's gender identity wasn't considered abuse, whereas our judge saw it as abusive when my ex-husband was refusing to call Greg by his name and pronouns, and not respecting his gender identity. That really helped me with terminating his rights and keeping Greg safe. I think that bill died. There was also some other ones. They tried to pass a trans sports ban that time, too, but it did not pass in 2019. There were a few like our state Equality group and our transgender group. They would send out emails or reach out when the state was trying to pass anti-gay and anti-trans bills, asking if we would come and testify. So we were doing that, and they also had a Capital Day in 2019, though it was just a bunch of LGBTQ+ folks.

We had a rally and caring legislators let the trans kids be official Pages for a day. They got to go down the House floor, to learn all about it. It's funny because the representative Greg was Page for is now our rep. We moved to her area, and she was amazing. She's a bisexual legislator. We got lots of pictures, lots of certificates. Greg knew more about the legislator after that day than I knew. So it was a learning experience. She and her office absolutely adored Greg and kept in touch. She wrote him a letter of recommendation to get him in college. We saw her a lot in the 2021 session too. She was there always on our side and helping out. But in 2019 it was like pre-COVID. We could go and meet people. By 2021, a lot of the state legislators considered COVID over. We are still trying to be masked and safe as possible because we didn't want to get sick.

In 2019, it was kind of scary testifying. I was nervous, but our reception was very welcoming. They were always very nice. In 2021, it was downright hostile and dangerous. We got doxxed after the 2021 session. People would drive by our house and my phone got thousands of phone calls a day. A lot of parents who testified in that session got death threats and rape threats as if we are child abusers or groomers.

I've had several instances of people trying to follow me to work so I've have to call the police. I'm a social worker; I'm not taking crazy people to my office. I'm from the Chicago area originally, so I would use my Chicago style driving to lose them in the city traffic because I didn't want to take these people to where I work. I would either have to lose them, or if I couldn't I'd have to call the cops them and ask them to meet me somewhere before I get to work. The cops would just talk to these guys. A couple of them got arrested for having guns they weren't supposed to have. Now I carry mace and a taser with me all the time.

I had a guy pull a gun on me, though he did get arrested. He was following me to work, so I pulled over. But he gets out and he has a gun in his hand. Terrified, I take off and I'm driving around until I see a cop at a Burger King parking lot. I pull in, jump out, and yell to him, "Please help me!" The guy pulls in right after me, jumps out of his car, and pulls his gun again. The cop ordered him to put his weapon down. Turns out he had a felony conviction or something so he wasn't allowed to carry in our open-carry state. So that's how he got arrested, not for harassing me but because he illegally had a gun. I believe they also charged him with assaulting a police officer because he pulled the gun on me and the cop.

I am sure Greg will make it to New Zealand, but I may not because I'm the groomer, I'm the pedophile, I'm the one with the target on my back. For a couple of months I was sure I was going to get killed one day. Greg is a child, so they don't want to hurt him. In their crazed mindset he's my victim, because I groomed him, I made him trans. It's me they want to hurt. If I get killed, at least my life insurance will help keep him secure in New Zealand. I do everything I can to be as safe as possible. I don't want to die. I want to get out of here, but I will keep my son safe.

It's like the crazies don't want me to show up for the 2023 session. They don't want me to keep talking to reporters or telling people my son is this amazing human being. That being trans has nothing to do with how amazing he is. They want to shut me up, but I won't. You're not going to stop me from defending my son's right to be himself. I don't know that we'll ever come back to the state, but I want to do as much as I can before we leave to make it as safe as possible for those we leave behind.

I don't know how it is to be safe. We haven't been safe in five years. I remember dropping him off in college last year at the dorm. All the other moms were crying and I didn't cry and everyone was expecting me to cry because I absolutely adore my child. But to me, he's safer there than he is with me. So I felt relief. When we move out of the state, I think we'll all feel relieved. I'm on antidepressants, I'm on an anti-anxiety meds. I don't know if it's safe even going to the grocery store anymore, so I order all my groceries delivered because I don't know if somebody might try to kill me.

We do have a gun. We keep it at home. I don't feel comfortable though. I'm afraid I would be the person who shot herself in the foot if I took it with me, so it's at home for protection. We have an alarm system, obviously, to know what's going on. The doxxing has faded because people are not coming by the house every day, and I'm not followed every time I go to work. But I still get a lot of death threats, which I forward, to the police.

I go to work, but that's about it. When my husband is with me, I feel safer. Nobody ever says shit to him because he's a scary looking guy. But if it's just me or Greg out, people will say shit to us. They're not scared of me. I'm five foot nothing, a tiny little person so they feel like it's okay to come up and say shit to me or my kid. I am a very social person. I like going out. I just went out with coworkers last Tuesday after work. But before we went to the place, I checked out the restaurant we were going to. I found a safe spot where I felt like I could park and get in and out quickly. Not that anyone was following me. I didn't notice that. It's just that now I always have to be on high alert. I'm always exhausted because this is constantly stressful. And I feel trapped. I don't really go many places because it's just not worth it.

Some people say to me, Greg's 18. Just send him to New Zealand. You don't have to move too. But why am I going to stay here? He's never going to come back and visit me, so I might as well go with him. He's my only child. He is my life. I will do anything for him. And if New Zealand is where I think we're going to be the safest and have the best bet at a good life and maybe some feeling of safety so we can finally relax, and then I'll do it. I don't care if he's 18 or 30.

Hopefully we are out of here in May or June, because school starts down there in July, which is their winter. So the earliest we can get our visas to allow us to be in New Zealand would be May. But it's really dependent on the house selling. It's on the market. We've had lots of interest, but we also can't put a For Sale sign in front of our house, because it would just bring more doxxing and other online abuse. Our realtor has set up all the showings because I need to make sure that anyone is pre-approved before they set foot in our house. Everyone keeps saying that I need to do an open house to build interest and get it sold, but I can't do an open house. Absolutely not. I'm not letting some random person come walking through my house because for all I know they're planting cameras. Not that we're interesting. We're not. That's why I tell people like, I don't know why you're so interested in me. I'm your typical boring American mom. I work, I watch some TV, I foster puppy dogs and cats, and when my kid comes out of his room we sometimes have some good conversations about nothing in particular.

When you're testifying, there's always supposed to be eight to 12 committee members, but they're never all there. Usually three or four committee members are there to hear testimony and they switch out. I've noticed them playing on their phone when you're talking. I want to say, You want to pass a law that harms my son, the least you could do is put your fricking phone down for two minutes and look at me, because you only get two minutes. They've asked dumb questions, because I testified about how Greg had top surgery and how it's been life saving for him. I don't think he could have gone much longer without it to be comfortable in his own body and shower with lights on. Absolutely lifesaving.

And then to be asked, *So you think it's lifesaving to mutilate little girl's breasts?* No. Top surgery is typically done on patients 18 or older. And doctors' gatekeeping comes with it. Letter from a psychiatrist. Letter from your doctor attesting to you living in your true identity for two or three years. There's all these hoops you have to jump through to get there. And once you get there, you're like, Yay! But they make it seem like you could walk into a plastic surgeons office with a five-year-old girl and have her breast tissue removed.

I've been having nightmares of Ted Cruz coming and taking my kid. I know it's not going to happen because Greg is 18, but still I dream of these Republican lawmakers passing these bills and the coming with pitchforks and chasing him out of town. Greg has night terrors where legislators give him back to his biological father and force him to detransition. Rationally, we know that's not going to happen, but they're trying to pass laws to say you can't be you. And of course my ex-husband is one of those people who would be calling my caring for Greg abuse. He said I was abusive the whole time. I was affirming Greg. So, yeah, even though we live in the blue-city bubble, Greg has fears of him or his partner being killed just because they went on a date. Four years ago, we moved here thinking we were going to finally be safe. But you're not safe in even this blue bubble. I mean, purple bubble. My friend called it a blue mirage, and I think that's right. You think it's blue, you think it's progressive, but even though you feel like it should be because it's a big progressive city, you're not really safe. If you're not safe in the big, blue cities, where are you safe?

To legislators I say, "Leave my kid alone. Leave our families alone. Fix the grid. Worry about fixing real problems in our state." My son is an amazing kid, and being trans is just one of many adjectives to describe him. We're not running around with a neon sign. He's just a normal 18-year-old boy. If you met him, you wouldn't know there's anything different from any other 18-year-old boy you met. I don't understand why you're trying to demonize these kids who are just trying to be kids. Honestly, every kid I know from the community is amazing and has all these wonderful attributes. Being trans is the least interesting thing about them. If I gave you a list of things about my kid, him being trans wouldn't make the list, because it's not that cool or important. It's not who he is.

Child Protective Services (CPS) has now investigated me 10 different times for 10 different charges. The tenth time CPS visited us was in March, 2022. Greg was living in another state at college when they showed up and asked to speak with him. I told them, "You must be mistaken, because he's an adult now." And she answered, "Oh, well, we had his age as under 18." I told her I would send his birth certificate. I had a lawyer because I knew this stuff could happen. She said CPS told her that the so-called abuse happened before Greg turned 18, so they could still investigate. So basically they were saying because as a social worker I work with children in disabled and vulnerable populations, they had to stop me and take away my career because I was abusing my child before he was 18.

The last investigation, which was the one after the Attorney General's non-binding opinion, was the one where they went after my career. I'm pretty sure it was my ex-husband and his family who made the charge that I was brainwashing him and forcing him to be trans. And then supposedly I also beat him with a baseball bat. So CPS came and investigated. Greg had some bruises because he fell down the stairs at our old house. The school had called me once because of the bruises. He told them that he fell down the stairs. But it was mostly the problem was, CPS never tells you who reports you. They asked Greg stuff like, "Did your mom make you be gay? Did your mom make you be a boy? Did your mom say you had to do this? Did your mom say you couldn't see your dad anymore? Has she ever beaten you with a baseball bat?"

We have what we call a safe folder. Most families of trans kids in this state do. Once I heard about them, we made a safe folder. It has letters from his therapists, doctors, stuff like that. Teachers, people who know me saying I'm a good mom and doctors saying that I didn't force this on him.

The first investigator said to me, "What you've done to your daughter is horrible." She was obviously biased. But she got removed from the case. The first two investigations happened in 2017 and 2018. They showed up on Mother's Day of 2018. Those two took the longest because of the baseball bat thing. The others were really quick because it was pretty much like same thing. They were like, "Oh, we already talked to you." But they'd come, I'd give them the safe folder, and then they'd double check the same things. They talked to Greg and it was pretty open and shut. They were aware that somebody'd been reporting us. But then it kind of stopped once Greg's custody hearing was done.

He turned 18 in February of 2022 and I remember making a big like Facebook post about it, like we're free. I don't have to ever worry about CPS showing up on my door again. He's an adult now so I can finally breathe a sigh of relief. And on March first, as I mentioned, a CPS person showed up at my front door asking to speak to my adult son. They said that they closed the case. My lawyer and I have been trying for the last three or four months to get documentation of that, but they have not sent us any documentation.

This last one, I believe, is because a gentleman got in my face at the Capitol and was trying to videotape my then minor son going to the boy's bathroom. I took his phone, deleted the footage off his phone, and basically told him to get lost. He didn't like me because I didn't take his shit. That had already gotten in trouble for threatening lots of trans families. The cops at the Capitol gave him back his phone and told him to leave us alone. But, that's one of the things they were investigating me for. It was after Greg was 17 that I supposedly beat him up while we were at the Capitol. Twelve people reported the same incident of me punching, kicking, and dragging Greg by his hair through the Capitol back in June of 2021. If that happened, why did it take them till March of 2022 to report it? And how would all the armed guards at the Capitol let me beat the crap out of this child and drag him away like nobody was going to stop me. How many witnesses would be at the Capitol if that had happened? But they said they had 12 reports of the same thing, from a group that calls itself The Women's Protection League.

So now that you can't go after my kid, you're going after my career. It took me a very long time to get through college and get this career. I worked really hard to be where I am. We're not going to lose it just because Republicans don't like me. I'm going to go and get my master's and then my Ph.D. and I'm going to make the world a better, safer place for kids like my son. I may have to do it from the safety of New Zealand, but I'm not going to stop fighting just because I fled. I hate the fact that I'm leaving, because I kind of feel like I'm quitting which makes me feel guilty. But I have to do what's best for my family. I deserve peace of mind, and my son deserves to be a teenager.

And it's getting worse. It's not getting better. I always hoped it was going to get better. It's not and I can't risk it anymore. We have done so much. We have given all we have to give. I can't keep asking my son to put his life at risk. Greg was talking to a friend who was sharing their fun high school memories. And Greg just looked at them and said, "My high school memories are testifying at the Capitol. That's all I know. When people ask me about high school, I tell I spent my entire high school career running up to the Capitol testifying for my life."

So no prom, no dances, none of that stuff. Greg's main high school memory was, "Please don't pass this law and kill me."

CHAPTER 2—AMBER

PARENT: Allison
Sexual Orientation: Straight
Gender Identity: Female
Age: 41

CHILD: Paula
Gender Identity: Trans Female
Pronouns: She/her
Sexual Orientation: Lesbian
Age: 7

> *"It took me four days to drive to Connecticut with three kids, four cats and three lizards (bearded dragons). We lived out of our van. If we had to go to the bathroom, I drive to the gas station. For food, we've been living meal to meal. At night, I park at a truck stop on the Interstate where there's someone on duty 24/7 and the kids just curl up in their seats to sleep. It's getting cold now, so I have to run the engine every now and then to keep us warm at night. But being here is still better than being back there."*

Christmas last year was the first time I realized that something was going on with Paula's gender. Before that I thought she was just going to grow up to be gay, and I was fine with that. She was always so angry and sad. She would cry and say, I just don't know what's wrong with me. I don't know what's wrong with me.

What's wrong with me? Then come Christmas, she asked Santa for a dress and high heels for her presents. Yeah, high heels. All the stuff she wanted for Christmas was girl stuff. She wanted a dollhouse, LOLs, lip gloss, you name it. Christmas morning came, and she was so excited. I've got a picture of her in her dress Christmas morning. She was so excited when she went and put it on.

All that week, she didn't want to take the dress off. Then, it was like the light came on. One day I looked at her and asked, Are you a boy or a girl? She told me, I'm a girl. Call me Crystal. I thought, That's what it is; that's what's been going on: she's *transgender*. All of a sudden I knew why she had been so angry, why she was so sad all the time, why she didn't like herself, why she was constantly asking for earrings, why she always wanted her nails polished and wanted lip gloss and makeup. My eyes were now open to what was going on.

I was like, Ok, let's do this! I didn't know what was entailed, or what was going to happen. And at that time, I hardly knew anything about the trans community. But I just thought, If this is what will make her happy, let's go, let's see what we need to do. That very day we went to Walmart and she got to pick out some dresses and panties and everything and had so much fun shopping. She was a totally different child after that. Happy-go-lucky, not sad anymore, not angry with herself. It was like she was just totally content with herself.

As far as her siblings, it was a little bit harder for Mitchell because Paula had always been Mitchell's brother and they shared a room together. Now all of a sudden, she's Paula. And Paula moved into Penny's room with her and had girl toys and everything. So it took a little adjusting for Mitchell to understand that Paula will still play with him, but now Paula is a girl.

Penny was pretty much smooth sailing. I moved Paula from the room she shared with Mitchell into Penny's room where all their girl stuff was, and they just went with it. They've all three adapted. Now if someone tries to call Paula him or he, or call her by her dead name, Mitchell and Paula jump right in and say, No, it's Paula, and it's she!

I ended up doing a lot of research over the past year to learn about transgender. I've done so much reading. I'm about three-fourths through a book called *How to Be a Girl* by Marlo Mack. It's written by another mom of a trans-daughter, about her experience with her daughter who was trying to express that she was a girl. At first, the only real knowledge I had was from the TV show *I am Jazz*, because the kids loved watching it. Also, my best friend and I loved going to drag shows on the weekends, and the bar manager where we went was trans. So I was slowly learning about what transgender was.

As far as telling family and friends, that occurred over the next week. The kids were out of school for the holidays, so I had time to figure that out. Two or three days later, I was like, Okay, now I've got to figure this out as far as how to tell people. I went from being excited and, Okay, Paula, you're happy now. You can be you! to thinking to myself, Oh God, how am I going to tell my family? What do I say? I was afraid, and worried. I didn't want anyone to make Paula feel uncomfortable.

I started with my family. Since it was the holidays, I figured I could call and say, Happy Holidays! Oh, and by the way.... My aunt and my best friend were the first two I told: So it turns out Paula is transgender, she wants to be called 'Paula' and basically she's a girl. I tried to explain to them a little bit of what trans was. My aunt has been A-Okay with it. My grandmother thinks it's a phase and that she's going to go back to being a boy.

They haven't quite completely gotten it, but they go along with it and call her Paula, so I'm not constantly having to correct them. My best friend was a little bit touch-and-go at first. But after she did some research on her own, she was very accepting of Paula. She messes up and calls her by her dead name every once in a while, but is always quick to correct herself and apologize.

The next person I told was my half-sister. She called me and I talked with her on the phone. I said, I'm sorry. I've been just a little bit distant. I didn't know how to explain to you about Paula. You know, Paula is trans. She's a girl. I wasn't sure you'd be accepting. And she said, Oh, no, I'm fine with it. I'm just glad she's happy. It was her who called CPS on us. I have not talked to her since.

Before that, we were always going over to see her. As often as I had a chance, I would take the kids over and we would spend the day. After that phone call, she avoided me. I didn't really catch on until later because she was avoiding us coming over. I would ask her, Hey, can we come over? You know, we don't got anything planned. Can we come over and spend the day.

And she would say, Oh, well, we've got such and such. We won't be around. Let's try another time. And then she would never reach back out. So a little later I'd try again.

Next thing I know, CPS was knocking at my door. I texted her and said, Someone called CPS on me. She just texted me back. Wow, really. She never asked me what was going on, or why CPS was called, which sounded a little fishy. I ended up getting a lawyer through Lambda Legal. They are the ones who pushed and found out a bit more. CPS didn't come straight out and say that it was my sister. But based on the evidence they gave, the only person it pointed to was her. She had apparently told them I was mentally ill and was making Paula be a girl. I had to go to my doctor and get a letter stating I was not mentally ill and not on any medications and submit it to CPS.

Then about a week after the case had been closed, I received my letter saying that it was closed. But then I started getting threatening text messages from my sister, saying things like, You should never have been a mother. I don't care what it takes. I'm going to take those damn kids away from you. Your mother would be disgusted with you. Just horrible stuff. That's when I knew without a doubt that it was her.

I had no warning whatsoever about that first CPS visit. A gentleman showed up at my door one day when I had COVID. I had Penny check the door because I thought it was my aunt who was supposed to be bringing me some soup. Penny went to the door and told me, Mom, there's a man here. So I got up and walked over, trying to stand back a little. I told him, I have COVID. I know you don't want to come in. He answered, It's okay. We can stand right here and talk at the door. I'm with Child Protective Services, and we have some allegations in regards to Matt, which was the name on their records. And I said, You mean Paula? And he said, Matt. I told him, It's Paula, she is transgender. I know that's why you're here because of Paula being transgender.

So I talked to him at the door for a bit. He said, I do need to physically see the kids. I don't need to talk to them. We can do that another time. I just need to take a picture showing that I did physically see the kids. So they walked outside so he could take a picture of them. Then he scheduled a time that he was going to come back a few weeks later, but he never showed up. And I thought, well, maybe they decided to drop it.

I was so naive. A little over a week after he was supposed to have come, he showed up at my door again, wanting to talk to Paula and my other kids, as well as me. I didn't know any better at the time, so of course I let him in. But what he didn't know is, I had a camera in my son's room. So when he went in there to talk to the kids by himself, I was actually watching. I was able to see everything. I tried to record it too, but the phone wouldn't let me record. He questioned each kid alone for about 15 minutes. He didn't ask the kids anything about Paula being transgender. He asked each of them if they knew what drugs were. I mean, those are leading questions, fishing for something. Then he asked them if they knew of anyone who did drugs. He asked them if they knew what alcohol was, and if they knew anyone who drank. Paula was kind of funny and said, "Yeah, I drink beer." I'm thinking, Oh my God, no. You drink root beer. Finally the CPS worker figured out what Paula was talking about. He asked her, You mean root beer? To which Paula replied, Yeah, beer. Root beer. It's a fizzy drink.

He went on to ask each of them if anyone had ever touched

them inappropriately; how many times there's people over at our house; if there are a lot of people randomly at our house; who would the kids go to if something bad was happening. He didn't ask any questions that had to do with Paula being trans, even though that's why he was there.

He stayed for about two hours, because he next talked to me for about an hour. He was just getting general information. Other people who could vouch for me, like my aunt. He asked for her phone number and everything. I also talked to him about my sister, not knowing at the time that it was my sister who had called CPS. I was talking about how wonderful my sister was, knowing now that he was probably thinking, Oh, she's the one who called you in. And I was telling him about how wonderful she was, how much I loved her and my brother-in-law. Are they ever around the kids?, he asked. Yeah, I said, we usually try to get together quite a bit. We haven't seen them in a while, though. Do you want her number? And his answer unintentionally tipped me off when he told me, No, I don't need her number.

I sent Amber Briggle a message that said, I just had CPS at my house. I don't know what to do. She said to call Lambda Legal and let them know what's going on. So the next morning I called Lambda and they sent me information about which lawyers were working with them. I got set up with one of the lawyers fighting for the trans community here right now. Derek told me not to let CPS come in again, not to talk to them again, and if they show up, to tell them to talk to my lawyer.

He basically handled everything after that. He told me that the allegations were that I was mentally ill. He asked, Do you have any mental illnesses whatsoever? I told him, No. I'm dealing with some anxiety and grief because my mom passed away a year ago. But I am not mentally ill. He told me, Well, the allegation is that you're mentally ill and that you are forcing Paula to be a girl. I need you to get a letter from your doctor stating that you're not mentally ill and that you're not on any medications. So I got with my doctor and had him write a letter for me. Then my lawyer got CPS to close the case. It was a big mess and just incredibly stressful.

Then my sister opened another case on me. It took me a while to get that one closed. And that's when I decided we're getting out of town. I could see they were going to continue investigating me and if even one of them went the wrong way, I could lose my children. So that week, with some help from my best friend, I sold everything I could, and we left. It took me four days of constant driving to get us to Connecticut.

When we were about nine hours from the Connecticut state border, I got a call from our lawyer who asked me, How close are you to Connecticut? I told him, We are about nine hours away right now. He asked, When did you leave the state? I told him, We left Sunday around 1:00. He said, There's a new case that's been opened up now, and its accusing you of going online and buying hormones illegally and giving them to Paula. All I could respond was, What?! Then he told me, I did some searching online to see if what it was even possible to do this. It is not. I don't know why CPS is investigating something that can't even be done. I am going to call and talk to the CPS agent and see what's going on, and then I'll give you a call back.

When he called me back, he asked me, How close to Connecticut are you now? And I said, A little over four hours. He said, Get your ass to Connecticut. I don't like the way this CPS agent is acting. We didn't make any more stops. We drove straight to Connecticut after that.

A few days later he contacted me to say this newest case was closed. I'd actually spoken with that CPS worker, because he called me and said he was trying to get the case closed. All he needed was confirmation that we were no longer in the state. I talked to him for a few minutes and told him, It's been suggested that I take out a restraining order against my sister. He said, I would recommend that. He didn't say out and out that it was my sister behind all this. But he was basically saying, Yeah, that's the best thing to do—put a restraining order against her.

I've looked into it, because I don't want her reaching out to any of us, trying to get information, or finding out where we are. But there's been so much other stuff going on. My sister works in the medical office where my best friend used to be a patient. She illegally went into my best friend's medical records to get her phone number. Then she started harassing her for my information. But my friend won't give her any information about where we are. My aunt has also refused to talk to my sister, or give her any kind of information. So right now, I'm just letting it be. If my sister finds out where we are and starts bothering us, then I'll pursue that restraining order.

Before all the issues with CPS, I had already started planning to leave the state. I was planning on Illinois. I had looked into what cities were good there, I'd started connecting with others through Facebook support groups for trans families to see what their thoughts were as to which areas were best for trans kids. But when all of the stuff with CPS happened, I talked with Kimberly S. who had already left the state with her kids and was here and she told me, I will tell you right now, there's only three states that have laws to protect us parents when it comes to the CPS, and that's Massachusetts, Connecticut, and California. Other than that, wherever you go, they can still send you back there. So I decided that we were coming here to Connecticut instead.

Pulling the kids from school wasn't hard, because the only one who was in public school when we left was Mitchell. A week before we left, I pulled him from school because I was so fearful of my half-sister showing up with the police and trying to take him from the school or something. So I kept him at home that last week before we actually left town. Penny and Paula were in a home schooling program because of the issues Paula was having at the end of the previous school year. I had changed to homeschooling her, so she wouldn't have to deal with the school not letting her use the girls' bathroom and also we wouldn't have to worry about the bullies.

Since Penny is so good with school, I gave her the choice:

Do you want to go back to school, or do you want to homeschool with Paula? She wanted to homeschool with Paula. The only thing Penny was upset about was she had to leave her Girl Scout troop. She's been corresponding through the mail and on Messenger with her friends, and she's also made some new friends here, which has helped.

When we got to Connecticut we didn't have a place to land per se. We were living out of our van. So to be able to get mail, and have an address, I got a P.O. box. By the Monday after we reached Connecticut, I had decided on where I wanted to settle and get a place. I called and talked to the school administrative office and told the person about what all had happened, that I had decided on settling in this town and I needed to get my kids enrolled. She was very sympathetic. She told me to just fill out the forms online. Everyone in the community has been very helpful here. Paula loves it here; she feels so accepted. Everyone knows her as Paula. She said the only person she told she was trans was her best friend.

We went back and forth between hotels and the van. Every week when I got paid, I would divvy up that money as far as what it goes to. Some of it goes toward us having a hotel for a night or two, part of it goes to gas, part of it for food. I would say on average, every four days, we were able to get a hotel room for the night, so we could take showers and have a good night's sleep.

From time to time we've had help with hotel stays, or someone has offered to let us stay with them for a few days. The rest of the time, we live in the van. If someone has to go to the bathroom or something, then I drive to a gas station. It's just what we've had to do. As for food, since we are in the van, we are living meal to meal. We do a lot of sandwiches, making sandwiches in the van because it's really cheap doing it that way. When we're in the hotel, we're able to get TV dinners and heat them up in the microwave.

In the evenings we would use Penny's phone and put on Netflix, Amazon Prime, or Disney. The phone, or TV gets turned off at 8:00 p.m. Then I put iHeart Radio lullabies on my phone, which they don't always like, but it helps them go to sleep. They just curl up in their chairs in the backseat and go to sleep. Penny goes to bed at 9:00 p.m. since she is older, so she usually plays games on her phone after the other two go to bed.

Once they are all asleep, I recline my seat just a little bit and I go to sleep. Every so often I wake up to look around and check things out. But when we are in the van I don't sleep really well. The most comfortable place I've found to park overnight is the truck stop in a neighboring town, just off the Interstate. I like it because there's a bathroom available and they have someone on duty 24/7 watching the area. I feel safest parking closest to the building and sleeping there.

On weekends, I try to keep them busy. Once they get up and eat something, I usually have them go change into some clean clothes and we go to the park. We've explored several of the parks within maybe a 25-mile radius of our new hometown. That's how I first figured out that I wanted to settle in our new town. We went to one of the parks in the area and I talked to some moms about the issues we were having, why we were in Connecticut, and they were really nice.

When we first got here, I contacted 211 and they connected me with an agency that could give us some help. They paid for us to stay in a hotel for about two-and-a-half-weeks. Then they connected me with The Friendship Center, which was supposed to help us find a permanent place. The woman at The Friendship Center was so flaky. One day she got my hopes up, and told me she had three places that I was going to get to see that day. I was so excited and told her whichever was the best fit, we would go with. Just so I could get us somewhere more permanent. She said, "Let me contact them and see what time we can see them today." I told her I had a meeting at 10:30, so I could see them before that or after 12 noon.

I didn't hear from her so after my meeting, close to noon, I called her. She's like, "Oh, I'm fixing to go to lunch. I'll reach out to them when I get back to the office and let you know when we can go see them today." I waited, and waited. At 3:00 I still had not heard so I called her again. When she answered I said I hadn't heard from you yet so I thought I would call you. She says, "Oh, I'm just about to clock out for the day." I'm thought to myself, What? What about these houses you told me we're going to go look at today? After that I started trying to contact places on my own. Which has been difficult, trying to do that and work with everything else.

It was really hard trying to find a place to live until December 5th. That morning I got a message from Carrie. She lives in Connecticut and does a lot of nonprofit stuff in her community as well as the LGBTQ+ community in Connecticut. She messaged me and said if I would come to Avon, she could get us in a hotel for several days? That was an offer I was not going to pass up. So we met her that afternoon at the Marriott Hotel in Avon. She had paid for the hotel until Thursday, and brought us some groceries. She also invited us to the tree lighting there in Avon that night. She wanted me to meet some people in the community.

The places we had been staying in were like $60, $70 a night. The Marriott is closer to $150 to $200 a night. Carrie and others in the community donated their Marriott points to keep us in a hotel, while she helped me find a place for us to live. The kids were convinced the hotel was an apartment. I told them, "No, this is a hotel, but a really nice one." We stayed there until we found a place. In a matter of a day Carrie found three places for us to check. The first was available to view at 6:30 that next day on Tuesday. I went and looked at it by myself. Then on Wednesday we met at 1:00 to look at another one. Then we met at 4:30 to check out the last one, and the last was the best of the three. So we jumped on it and put in the application the very next day.

We ended up with around $4,800 donated from the community through Carrie's help to get us in a place and help us pay the first month's rent. Once I had been approved, Carrie had me make a list of things we needed. So I went to Walmart and made her a list. She posted the list to the community, and texted me a few hours after and said almost everything had been claimed that someone was going to get for us. When it came to moving us in, Carrie and some friends helped me move in and put furniture together. The love I have received from our new community has been unbelievable.

The atmosphere is definitely different from back home.. If I could talk to the state politicians who did this to us, I would tell them to go fuck themselves. My daughter should never have had to deal with this [crying]. She should have been able to live her life where she wanted to and be herself.

To other parents in my situation—even though sometimes you feel like you're alone, it's just a matter of seeking out, and reaching out to others that are going through the same thing. Because with me, Kimberly, has been a godsend. Having her to vent to and have her listen. Someone who is going through the same thing. I need our back-and-forth. It's just a matter of finding someone in your community who's right there with you, because they're going through the same thing. I just don't get those parents who aren't accepting. Why would you not want your child to be happy? Why would you purposely want to hurt them by not accepting who they truly are? As for me, I will move mountains to insure my kids are safe and happy.

CHAPTER 3—KAYLEE

PARENT: Kaylee
Sexual Orientation: Straight
Gender Identity: Female
Age: 52

CHILD: Chloe
Gender Identity: Trans Female
Pronouns: She/her
Sexual Orientation: Pansexual
Age: 12

> *"If it had not been for Chloe, I could have been one of those people attacking the Capitol on January 6th. That's how my family is. I was an ordained minister at the time, and I spent the better part of a year making Chloe's life horrible doing what I thought was right. Chloe was only three or four, but everyone thought the devil was trying to use her for evil. After a year of conversion therapy, she was praying to go to heaven and be with Jesus, so she could be a girl. She would rather go to heaven and be with Jesus and live as herself for eternity, than stay here and live as boy one more day."*

I knew Chloe was different. I just always knew she was different, though I couldn't put my finger on it at first. By the time Chloe was 18-months-old her mannerisms and her preferences were all very feminine. It was very obvious. When I look back at pictures now, you can see in the photos how seemingly feminine she was. When she was old enough to have the language to express herself, she realized that the people around her didn't know she was a girl, so she started saying it to everyone: *You know I'm a girl.*

I was an ordained minister at the time at a church. We tried to get her what we thought was help: psychologists, a psychiatrist, and conversion "therapy" for a year. We were still using her deadname and old pronouns, and encouraging her to be a boy. She would say at least six times a day, "I'm a girl in here," and I'd end up spanking her and yelling at her and saying endless prayers that she would change, because that was conversion therapy. So I spent the better part of a year making Chloe's life horrible and my life horrible doing what I thought was the right thing. We tried church ministries—one for personal crises like divorce or chronic illness and then another which exorcises and or "passed out" demons. Chloe was only three or four but everyone thought the devil was trying to use her for evil. After a year of this, she was praying to go to heaven and be with Jesus, so she could be a girl. She would rather go to heaven and be with Jesus and live as herself for eternity, than stay here and live as boy one more day.

That was when I realized I needed to start listening to my science brain instead of my religious brain. I started seeking help outside of the church and Christian counselors and Christian psychiatrists and Christian psychologists.

When Chloe came out to us, I didn't even know what *transgender* was. And the only thing I knew about gay was that these LGBTQ+ people were choosing to do things outside the will of God, and so they were all going to burn in hell. Because that's what I was taught by the church. But the education background I have in psychology, health, and science slowly began to conflict with my faith. It took me a long time to work through that conflict. For the past eight years I've told anyone who would listen that Chloe's not the one who transitioned, it was me. I'm different today, but she's always been just Chloe.

Chloe never hated her body. She doesn't think she was "born in the wrong body." She thinks she has a transgender girl's body, is perfect as a trans girl's body. She never told me she was gay, just that she was a girl. She wants boobs one day, and we've negotiated that. I told her, I'll help you buy boobs later in life if you need them. I am well-endowed. And Chloe's problem is that she's the biggest Shania Twain fan on the planet and she wants Shania Twain boobs. I'm not giving her any bigger boobs than I gave her older sister genetically. So I told her, if you want that, you have to get a job and pay for it yourself.

We didn't know any other people like us who were strong in their faith but who also knew that Jesus wouldn't want us being assholes to our kids. The science says that Chloe was born a trans girl. So why would God make her that way, if He wanted us to be horrible to her? Why would he want us to punish her? If people are born this way, how can we say that it's wrong?

I don't have a family anymore. My mom doesn't speak to me. My sisters won't speak to me. My aunts and uncles and cousins all have been pretty fucking horrible. I lost my grandparents. I was told not to attend my grandfather's funeral. I was written out of my parent's will. That best friend whose wedding I performed at, and whose delivery room I was in for both of her babies? She stopped talking to me cold. Close friends for the past 25 or 30 years disappeared on me instantly. No one returns my phone calls or my text messages. No more play dates for Chloe. Neighbors and random people hated me. I was getting it from the church, I was getting it from some LGBTQ+ activists, I was getting it from the school, and I was getting it on my job. I lost ministries that I had started. I was constantly under attack. All because I refused to turn my back on my daughter or denounce her as a sinner.

I have one cousin who grew up in San Francisco, who's my age and we stay in touch. And also my brother, who just came out last year at Thanksgiving, which is also my birthday. He came at 58-years-old and he told us that he did it because Chloe had

43

encouraged him. He said if she could go through what we've been through, then he could come out. For the first time in his life he felt that he would be supported by me and my kids who support Chloe.

We don't talk much about Chloe's siblings because I'm working really hard to maintain whatever relationship we have left. Her younger siblings had no trouble with her being their sister at all. They got her pronouns and name right away. They've loved and supported her every step of the way. My older kids started out supportive in the beginning, but the disinformation campaign is so strong now with their lies about blockers and cross-sex hormones are so well-coordinated now that they're struggling and we're just trying to hold that part of the family together as best we can. I'm just trying to keep my kids and grandkids together and moving forward as a family unit.

I'm no longer holding out for the rest of my family to come around. I don't even want them to come around anymore. I don't keep up with them. I don't communicate with them. It took a lot of healing and it was a long walk, but today breaking free of my family has been the best thing that's ever happened for me. If it had not been for Chloe and the journey that we've been on, I could have been one of those people attacking the Capitol on January 6th—that's the mindset of the family I was raised in. I'm no longer that person, but I would still be if it hadn't been for Chloe.

The people that stuck with me and encouraged and supported me and let me take my own journey are the people who saved Chloe's life. Especially Chloe's transgender *aunties,* who have been with her every step of the way. We were fortunate to have transgender people who stepped forward and answered the most offensive fucking questions I could ever ask them, and answered totally honestly, and continued to be there, no matter how much they hated how I was being a mother to Chloe. And they saved her.

I never wanted to be a public figure. But I've never shied away from it, either. It just kind of happened to us. It started when our school superintendent started talking to the media about my kid. Not by name of course. But in a small town, it didn't take long for everybody to figure out it was us. He kept talking to the media and publicly comparing my little girl to *pedophilia* and *bestiality*. I'm not going to let anybody just continue doing something like that and let it go unchallenged. The way I see it, I'm 52 and I am not going to be here forever, so I need to do as much as I can to make the world a better place for my kid before I'm not here to shield her anymore. That was my only goal in being so public.

We've gotten a shit storm of abuse every time I speak out, especially with me coming out saying, *I'm a Christian and I was a Republican.* It just brings more death threats. The major hate groups now have videos online of Chloe. But I know we're also educating people, and bringing more people to this fight who might otherwise not be there, so it's worth it.

At my first press conference, I told people that I'm a Christian, and I'm sorry for the things I've done to the queer community in the name of God. That shook a lot of people to the core. They had not heard anybody say that before. That was seven years ago and after that we had to move within our small town. Then we had to move again within our town. The people I was renting from had to put me in a different rental property and had to keep all the utility bills in their names, because so many people were threatening us online. Even some of my own family were threatening us online. So we moved and moved and moved within our conservative little town. Finally, it wasn't safe for us anymore, and we had to move to Dallas. It's supposed to be more liberal, but even there we weren't safe.

Once I was known, just going out for the most routine trips could be dangerous. I would be at the grocery store, picking something up, and someone would recognize us and start screaming at me. Back then we weren't being called *groomers* and *pedophiles* yet. But they'd accuse me of letting the devil have our children. They yell things like, *It's just really horrible that you're not trying to save your family. We don't want your kid in our school.* And, *You all need to get your kid out of our town.* Then when I was spit at on my way into in a Sam's Club, and I was like, *Yeah, this shit's done. I can't do this shit no more.*

I'm no longer in the Christian ministry. I now think organized religion is the worst thing that ever happened. But Chloe has made me stronger in my faith with the Jesus I serve than ever. It's sweet and it's comforting, and it gives me strength and hope. I've learned to not walk up to people and say, *You wouldn't be having problems if you were a Christian*—which is what as evangelicals tend to do. I can say that because that's who I used to be. I now know from the inside how horrible that can be. Chloe's made me a better mom, a better human, and a better Christian than I ever was.

I would say Chloe's whole journey has been what I would consider in my faith *divinely appointed.* My faith transitioned right before the North Carolina bathroom bill, when Chloe was in kindergarten, and the state was considering its own bathroom bill. It was then that 17-year-old Leelah Alcorn stepped out in front of a truck in Cincinnati, Ohio. In her goodbye note online, she wrote about her Christian parents. She said her mom had told her, "I would never truly be a girl, that God doesn't make mistakes, that I am wrong. If you are reading this, parents, please don't tell this to your kids. Even if you are Christian or are against transgender people don't ever say that to someone, especially your kid… The only way I will rest in peace is if one day transgender people aren't treated the way I was… My death needs to mean something."

Now *how* am I supposed to ignore *that*, when I'm looking at a kid who's telling me that she's a girl too? I looked at that note and it was like it was divine, like I was meant to read Leelah'a letter. I knew she was speaking directly to me. I consider Leelah very important in Chloe's life and me accepting her again. Leelah Alcorn stepped in to help us: she left that that suicide note, and it helped my daughter.

I've had to leave the state entirely to move to California. I lost my job. I lost all my retirement savings. I lost my ass selling our house. We came here with only what we could fit in the car. I said, *Fuck it, we will live in a tent if we have to. I am not waiting another minute. I'm not waiting because it's going to be too late.* When we planned our trip, we had to depend on donations from a few friends and lots of sympathetic strangers. I didn't have the money for us to stay at hotels. I had three cats and a dog and kids in the car and it's a long drive. A trucker had told me to stop and find a truck stop every 300 miles, fill up on gas, use the bathroom, get a snack, and then go sleep in the car. When you wake up, get back on the road, drive another 300 miles, and repeat it all over again.

And that's just what I did. It took two-and-a-half days driving straight through. I tried to make it fun for the kids. I bought them all road trip activities and had the back seat all set up for them with iPads and cell phones. They talked with reporters the whole way here, doing interviews from the back seat and making videos for the news crew that was tracking us. They'd wanted to follow us, but I told them, "No, you're not slowing me down. I don't have time for y'all. If you can find us on the road, you find us. But I'm not meeting y'all. I'm not slowing down. I have a goal to make." So the kids were sending them videos as we went, and we just kept hauling ass till we got here.

The donations from friends are all gone, without my retirement I only have two months' worth of savings, the new job I got here ends in February, and I only have my apartment through April. California may be a sanctuary state, but nothing is affordable. Rentals are hard to come by. My electric bill is double what it was back home, and I pay double here for half as much space in our apartment. You either have to be incredibly wealthy or poor enough to get assistance, because there's almost no middle ground for a single income family like ours. It's safe here, but financially it's just totally devastating.

After April we may end up living in our car. But I don't care. Even if we do, I'm never going back there.

We've started working with an immigration attorney to explore our options, because Republicans are talking about passing national anti-trans legislation in 2024, using the playbook from Florida and Texas.

When Chloe found out that the latest bill in this last legislative session would make it a felony offense to affirm your trans-kid, I told her, *Let's just take a break because my hair is falling out.* I had big chunks of bald spots and my belly was huge because my cortisol levels are always elevated. I told her, *Let's just sit out this legislative session. We'll work the social media and promote it as much as we can online, but I don't want to go to the Capitol again. I need a break.*

But that bill directly attacking parents was what lit a real fire under Chloe. She testified in front of the legislature and hasn't looked back since, She knows my rules for her as a public activist: *When you start thinking like a victim, I will not allow her to do this anymore. You are no one's victim. And you will stay kind and you will stay humble.*

To those religious Christians opposed to us, I would say that if they are people of faith, surely have read the Scripture that says, *Lord, Lord, did we not do all these things in Your name?* And the Lord looks at them and says, *I never even knew you.*

Scripture says we're supposed to work out our own faith with fear and trembling, because we can't judge other people, lest we become Pharisees, which the Bible warns about much more than it warns about being gay. In fact, it doesn't warn about being gay at all, but it does warn about being a Pharisee. So that's what I would tell these Christians who oppose us: *Walk the faith you claim to have, work out your own faith, and serve God.*

When you have a bad infection and the doctor gives you an antibiotic, they always say, *You might feel worse initially because as the antibiotic is trying to kill off your infection, your infection is going to fight to stay alive. But you have to keep going because ultimately you're going to get rid of the infection.* That is what I see with racism and homophobia and transphobia. It seems worse right now, because we're in the spotlight, we're the people in this particular time in history fighting the bad infection. And it will seem to get a lot worse, but in the end we'll do it and we'll leave a better world for our kids coming after us.

CHAPTER 4—JUNO

PARENT: Juno
Sexual Orientation: Straight
Gender Identity: Female
Age: 50

CHILD 1: George
CHILD 2: Findlay
Gender Identity: Nonbinary
Gender Identity: Trans Female
Pronouns: He/him/they
Pronouns: She/her
Sexual Orientation: Asexual
Sexual Orientation: Pansexual
Age: 18
Age: 16

> *"It was always an abusive relationship, but it took my daughter coming out for me to realize how bad abusive it was. My husband has a lot of guns. He loves his guns. And if there's a domestic assault, he knew they'll take your guns. So after that, I wasn't really worried about anything physical, because his guns mean more to him than anything, He wanted me to choose between him and the kids. Well, I chose our kids."*

When George was 11, I wanted to do a special thing for him getting a period. So I went to get him a haircut and… Actually, I should go back a little further. There're just a lot of little spots, you know? Around nine, he came out dressed in his sibling's night costume, and had this mean face. He said, "I'm not a princess today," or something like that, which was a bit different from what he normally did.

The biggest thing was his period. I never got anything special when I was got mine, so I decided that we're going to get him a haircut and do all the female things. It'll be really special, I thought, which is a basic parenting mistake where you do for your child what you would have liked to have been done for you as a child. When I took him to get a haircut, the lady didn't listen to him. She gave him this very short cut—basically a bob. It was like a typical *Karen* haircut. He was very upset. It wasn't a fun day. I ended up cutting his hair shorter for him. And then every haircut he had after that got shorter and shorter. He came out as bi shortly after that. With him it was a very slow progression.

"Now I'm wearing men's clothing to high school, and I only want men's shoes..." It was so slow, so gradual. Just one thing after another. And then, all of a sudden, George is totally presenting as a boy. George was having an argument with his dad and he came down and handed me this note that read, "I would make a great son."

I had a friend who was trans who said maybe I should start calling George *he*. That's when I officially started using *him*. His name was Freya and he didn't like it. It made him feel icky. But he couldn't find a name he liked. So I said, "Why don't we just call you *George*? It'll just be a nickname until you figure it out. When you find your name, we'll start calling you that." That's what all his friends started calling him.

Once we accepted George as masculine, he went to the prom. The school had a gay prom and he went to that in a dress. So very occasionally he does feminine stuff, but he is mostly masculine. He says he's binary, but very masculine and he wants to get top surgery.

We didn't catch on to hormone blockers early enough because the transition process was so slow and it took him a long time to figure it out. Also he developed very early and I feel bad about that part. George didn't ask for blockers, though, and he didn't really mention it until he was 18.

I'd already been through it with Findlay. So I knew that's not really going to do anything for you. George wanted to do testosterone, but he was hesitant to start, because he really didn't want bottom growth. He basically really doesn't like the kind of genitalia that are available. He just doesn't want anything. Not the top stuff, like chest hair or beard or muscles. He just wants to be genderless. He doesn't want to be perceived as a man or a woman, which is kind of hard to explain.

When he was in elementary school, George was more feminine than he was in junior high. But then he switched when he was in high school. Any time he was perceived as a man, he was very happy. He looked more masculine, so people often took him as male. His happiest moments were when he was taken as male. He was talking about not wearing his binder. Some days he had boobs and another kid said to him, "So, why do you put on inflatable boobs?" He was so happy— *Oh, he thinks I'm a guy.*

Binding caused him problems with his breathing. So now he really wants top surgery. Even just walking down to his job with the binder on, which was fairly close, it would be tight and cause him problems. So now he only wears it on occasion and we're looking for a doctor.

I feel really bad for George because we're in a flux state because of this bad divorce I'm having. I'm just trying to figure out the insurance and things out. I push his dad to help pay, but he's totally anti-trans and George's insurance is under his dad's name which puts me in an awkward spot. *How can I do this? How can I help him get top surgery and pay for all this stuff?*

It will be difficult to get reimbursed if dad doesn't support it. Technically, I guess it doesn't make any difference, as long as insurance supports it. But as a practical matter, I'm sure it's difficult. I can't push his dad too much, because I don't want him pushing back on the hormone blockers for George's sister,

Findlay. There's a mixed bag of what I can do, especially here in Idaho.

They changed the law so medical providers can't help trans kids here. But I'm going outside Idaho. And we're moving soon. We're working on getting top surgery this year and I'm going to see about doing a low dose of puberty blockers so that he doesn't have the bottom growth. That's our goal for this year.

His transition hasn't been all smooth sailing. We've had an extreme amount of conflict. He was sexually assaulted at his school. George got really depressed. Then this boy kept poking at George's boobs and making inappropriate comments for weeks. The school had the police officer at the school, the Resource Officer, tell this kid that if he ever did that again, the school would press charges. He was supposed to write a letter to George, which he never did. He was suspended for two weeks and that was it. When George went to school the next semester, that kid was in two of his classes. George just couldn't take it mentally. The school said, "Well, you can get out of it. You can leave these classes." They wouldn't remove that kid, And so George ended up leaving those classes..

Other kids felt empowered to harass and bully the kids who were gay or trans. His school basically did nothing. George kept trying to go to the principal and we kept talking to them but they were doing nothing. The principal's said, "No, it's both sides, it's two-sided thing, and it can't be the fault of one side or the other." If you look it up, there is an article online, I think in the *Times,* about a Hispanic girl who went to our school. Right before the Trump presidency, someone wrote a bunch of slurs on her car. That's the high school he was at.

So George tried to change things on his own. He gave kids lectures. But they were afraid of him because he was so vocal about everything. And it put an enormous amount of stress on him because he's not really very vocal. But he was also trying to protect all the kids around him. He was going out on a limb trying to protect these kids. He's just an amazing person. He connects to all these people. He talks to everybody and he has a lot of charisma. He talks to so many people that they formed a group. All the gay kids would sit at one place in the high school. Other kids who were against them would try to come and do stuff to them. The kids kicked a trans friend. One of the kids kicked George. In a blind rage, he went over to the group of kids and gave them a huge lecture about how they would not do that to his friend or other students. It was a big group of football players who were way bigger than George. The other kids were scared for George, so they held him off. The school didn't tell me anything about. The other kids got a slap on the wrist like, being told not to kick people.

It was just too much. He had all these kids he felt like he had to stand up to. Then outside of school at work nobody would talk to him because he was in a very male-centric job as a lifeguard. They wouldn't talk to him because they perceived him as different. And he's a very friendly kid. He kept trying to talk to them. So he ended up both quitting his job *and* leaving school. It just wiped him out mentally. Eventually it was so traumatic for George, that we took him out of school and he's now getting his GED. He was suicidal for a while between the bullying and the school's non-response and the sexual assault all happening at the same time He's under psychiatric care. We're trying to get him back on track, but a lot of devastating things happened all at once for the poor kid. At the same time, his dad was completely losing his shit over his sister.

With Findlay, the first thing we noticed was that she and her sibling would dress up. They like to put on princess dresses and spin to the music. I thought, *Okay, that's cool. Whatever my kids enjoy.* But their dad couldn't handle it. He said something to Findlay. Findlay would still wear the fairy rings, but she stopped dressing like a girl. This was when they were really little, from two up to four or five. Then, I think somebody said something to her and she's a sensitive kid. So she started doing boy stuff until about age nine.

Findlay mentioned once that she wanted a haircut like Tintin, while her dad really wanted her to have a traditional male haircut. I told her, "You should get your hair cut like Tintin, that would be great." I thought that if she was having a struggle with other kids, maybe it would help her. So we got her the Tintin haircut. I didn't know how short it was going to be when I went to pick Findlay up at the barbershop. She was devastated because, her hair had always been longish and curly. She was wearing her hoodie up. I said, "You look so handsome. You got your Tintin haircut. This is great." But she was devastated. She pulled her hoodie on tight all around her face. She went home and hid under their covers for hours.

When Findlay was nine she had beautiful curly light blonde hair. I didn't make her get her haircut, but I would ask her, "Let me cut your hair because it's curly. It's easy to cut if it's curly." But I'm not a very good stylist, so she'd always end up with these kind of little bob haircuts. People kept calling her a girl, and I thought, *Oh, that's got to be embarrassing for her.* So I'd always ask if she wanted me to cut her hair. "Do you want it to be shorter?" And she would always say, "No, it's fine."

She didn't mind if people called her a girl. Through her teen years, she went through a very anti-feminist time, probably six months of being very anti-feminist and being into guns, because her dad was really into his guns.

I kept thinking, something's up with Findlay. I just had this feeling. By that time, because George was bi, I had joined parenting groups and I was reading a lot of the stuff about moms with trans kids and a lot of it sounded familiar. But I didn't say anything. I tried to be positive about it.

When Findlay was 13, we were on a walk and she said, "Mom, I'm really a girl. I think that's why my hair was always such a big deal." I felt so bad. Somewhere I always knew. I just knew it, and I thought, *My God, I missed the opportunity to put her on blockers.* I was devastated, because I had missed all these opportunities. Maybe if I had said something, she would have come out sooner. I blame myself big time for that. I felt like I totally failed her.

Once she was girl-identified, she just totally switched. It wasn't like George, who was super gradual in his transitioning. It was like, *Now I'm a girl.* And we switched to a girl name and girl pronouns overnight.

Findlay was still totally in the closet to everybody, except the family. I had homeschooled her before this. I had chosen a secular homeschool group for her to hang out with. It wasn't as much pressure, not as many kids. I homeschooled her until she was in grade school, so she didn't have to experience public schools until seventh grade, when we put her back in the same school as George. Needless to say, it was not a welcoming school and she mostly stayed totally in the closet.

She kind of didn't need to come out in high school because George had such a big mouth and told a lot of people, anybody he thought that would be supportive of them: "Hey, my sister's trans." A couple of teachers knew and were supportive, and a couple of kids knew and they were supportive. But Findlay still presented as male, so nobody else knew and she didn't have to deal with the same crap as George. But she became suicidal too, because of all the crap she was hearing, like heard a lot of kids saying FS.

Findlay is neurodivergent. She's autistic and has a hard time with noise in school. So I ended up taking her out of school again, and now she's doing an online high school.

Dad was having a very hard time with this. I thought I could convince him. I thought he was somewhat on the same page. I thought he was an atheist, that he was more tolerant. But he was very proud of Findlay as a son. Any time her gender came up, he would just break down and sob and sob. I thought he was just doing it around me, but he was doing around George and Findlay, too.

He's also very sexist, which took me a long time to realize. He definitely had a favorite, and it wasn't George—it was Findlay. He wanted this really tall son. He was so proud he was going to have a tall son. He was always measuring Findlay when she was younger and saying things like, "Oh, you're going to be as tall as me." My ex-husband is six foot four, so he was so excited that she was getting tall. I think it ruined his idea of the kid he wanted. She's really into history so she and Dad talked a lot about history. She was trying to please him at one point and got into the guns for a little while and he was so proud of that.

Ours was always an abusive relationship and it took my daughter Findlay coming out for me to realize how abusive it was. So in a way, her transition freed me. Dad wanted me to choose between him and the kids. He wanted me to take her for a psychological evaluation and all this stuff and I refused.

Well, I chose our kids. I didn't even realize all the pain I was in. until I got away from him and could think.

In the meantime, he created a real shit storm. There were a lot of fights. He told Findlay that she would never be a *real woman.* He told me this trans thing was why she was suicidal. I kept trying to tell him that when kids are accepted, they're *less* suicidal. I went to my parents group and asked, "What can I do with this? My husband is just so anti-trans." They said, "Give him statistics. Give him all the information you can."

So I kept giving Dad information and talking to him and he would answer with a shit storm of horrible anti-trans things. Eventually I decided not to listen to his anti-trans rants anymore. He told me that it was the same as someone demanding that their hand be cut off and their eye gouged out because they though they were a pirate. He had been seeing this doctor at the VA who was anti-trans and suggested that my husband get her psychological help and gave him pamphlets. He hid these in the car's glove box. I found them there and I was so pissed. He was secretly reading this material from the VA doctor, but not sharing it with the kids.

We were a united front at home, where we tiptoed around the issue. I got a counselor and she was very pro-trans and helpful. She said, "Don't talk about trans issues around him at home." So we were trying not to talk about stuff. But the kids talk about stuff amongst themselves. He was losing his mind when we even brought it up. We couldn't bring up anything about gay or trans or he would just lose it. He would just sob and sob. And then he would just stop talking to me, and give me the silent treatment. It's hard to talk to someone when they're giving you the silent treatment.

I think he was having a religious trauma. His own dad is gay, but he never came out. It was always kind of a weird secret. We all knew he was gay and he was living with a man. I was okay with it. I explained it to the kids. But my husband never accepted his father. I don't know if that was part of it,

I took Findlay to a counselor and she said we might want to consider doing hormone blockers. I put it off for probably a month or two longer. I feel bad about that. But I knew that I was going to have to get Dad to agree to it. That's when he went to VA, and then threw a complete shit fit. He said, "We need to go to someone who has a better degree. That counselor doesn't have a degree." So I said, "But our doctor does. Our doctor's actually a doctor." So I dragged him to our doctor and she said, "This is how it works. If you get these kids on blockers they're more likely to survive. It'll give you and her a little time to know, to be sure." Then I said, "Okay, this is the best thing for our kid." I basically pushed through and got on the waiting list for blockers. I called a gender hospital in Seattle. We got the insurance. The hospital assured me that, if I was going to have problems, they would get me financial assistance.

My husband told me he was going to stop me. But I just railroaded this whole thing through. I got the doctors, I made the appointments, I went to Seattle, I got Findlay on blockers. And I basically ruined my relationship with him. But I couldn't wait any longer because Findlay was worried that she would get an Adam's apple and she was worried about growth, and even if I'd waited, he was never going to come around. I've been married to the man for 30 years. I knew he wasn't going to give in.

My main worry was that we'd waited too long. So I said, "This is the best thing." We went to the doctor and he wasn't going to stop me. He said, "I disagree with this, but if you need to do it, go ahead." I guess he thought I wouldn't actually do it. But I did, and once Findlay was on the blockers, he got really angry. Slamming doors. Not talking to me. Glaring at me. Any time I would come into the room, he would make this disgusted sound. It was this constant passive/aggressive storm.

I would have to go to work and I was desperate because my kids had to be there alone in the house with him. I would try to make other arrangements. so they could be at their friend's house. But inevitably they had to be by themselves with Dad. And then they would all get into big argument when I wasn't there. At one point he even tried to hit Findlay. George got in between him and Findlay, and told him that, if he ever did that again, he would call the police. He'd also threatened to hit George, but I didn't know about this until much later. Dad was giving him a long, drawn-out lecture and George told him to stop. He held his hand out like he was going to hit George. He also did this to the family cat. It was like a switch flipped and he just lost his mind completely. Over hormone blockers!

Now my husband has a lot of guns. He loves his guns, which is very common in Idaho. And if there's a domestic assault, he knew they'll take your guns in a domestic abuse case. So after that, I wasn't really worried, because he's so paranoid. His guns mean more to him than anything, so I felt fairly confident that he wouldn't do anything physical again. But after that, I asked him to move out. It took him a long time to find an apartment, but eventually he did.

He blamed everything, all of it, on me—I had ruined his dream. I kept asking him, "What do you want me to do? What was it that you wanted me to do?" And he had no answer. He'd just say, "Not this." He wouldn't use the right pronouns, and anytime I would say *she*, he would glare at me.

The kids dropped all contact with him. But he was scared of George after George threatened to call the police on him. So he didn't insist on contacting them.

I'd been married to this man since I was 19; I've been with him since I was 16. Now anytime I know my ex is coming over, I warn George and he stays in his room. He has flashbacks. George's dream is to become an animator, drawing and doing story animation. But we had to reorganize the computer room so nobody could stand behind him, because his dad would stand around behind him asking things like, "What are you watching? What are you doing?" We had to do the same with the dining room, so Findlay wouldn't have anybody walk up behind her like her dad.

I would definitely say they have PTSD from him. We had to go to back by the school for George to meet one of his friends, and when he went back in that high school, he just couldn't handle it. George can't be alone. He's always got to have a friend over or he's texting me. If he's alone, he draws for hours to cope with the stress of it all. He always has to play a game on his phone. He copes by playing those tap-tap games and he copes by listening to true crime stories. He has a problem sleeping. He doesn't get to sleep till like 2:00 a.m. And he has panic attacks. If it's a situation that reminds him of his dad, his jaw will tilt and his hands shake. If anyone walks up behind him, he kind of jumps. It a startle response.

With Findlay, she does it by isolating herself. She has a friend that I take her to see at the friend's house. She goes over there once a week for the day. She talks to her friend constantly and plays video games with him. She deals with her stress by listening to music and pacing. She paces at night, not going to bed at like 3:00 a.m. Findlay also has migraines. When she started school, she got horrible migraines and it was probably due to her dad losing his mind. So she has the pacing and listening to music and isolating herself. I'm trying to get her involved in some flag groups.???? PFLAG??

They're both on a lot of medication, which her dad was against, which is ironic because he's the main reason for it. George is taking antidepressants, which help him not have those panic attacks. He was having 10 or more a day. But since Dad moved out and we got him on the meds, his attacks have decreased and he just has them occasionally—like when Dad comes over or another situation stresses him out.

We're moving to Washington State, to Pullman, a college town 45 minutes away where I was able to find an apartment. We're lucky we live in the Idaho "chimney" in the north, so a blue state line is just a 20-minute drive. There was another town even closer, but it's very Trumpy; Pullman is just a bit farther and it's very liberal. Now I'm trying to find a job there. I'm still working part-time at my job in Clarkston, Washington, just over the bridge from Idaho. I can drive them down to see their friends, because I'm working twice a week down here.

If I had a message for the lawmakers in Idaho, I would ask them to protect trans kids. They're just trying to live their lives. They just want to live. You need to protect all kids, not just the straight ones. Some of their families have been here for generations; these kids are part of our state. They shouldn't have to move just because you're passing stupid laws to scare them.

To mothers who are wrestling with a transphobic spouse, I would say, "Protect your kids and protect yourself. And know the relationship might not work out. It's hard. Get yourself into counseling. But please know that nobody is going to be there for your kids but you. So *you* have to protect them. And if it comes to it, move away from your spouse. Make a plan, be proactive, and get away as soon as possible, because it's not worth languishing in a bad or abusive marriage. You might think you can change them, but if it goes beyond a couple of months you need to act. Yes, your spouse can change. But chances are they're not going to. And maybe they need to work on themselves away from the family anyway.

Today I wish I would have figured that out and gotten my shit together earlier. But that's been my journey. And I chose my kids and I've never regretted it for a minute.

CHAPTER 5—KAY

PARENT: Kay
Sexual Orientation: Straight
Gender Identity: Female
Pronouns: She/her
Age: 58

CHILD NAME: Kate
Sexual Orientation: Lesbian
Gender Identity: Trans Female
Pronouns: She/her
Age: 15

> *"We were on Main Street in the busiest part of downtown. And she's in tears. My whole world stopped and cracked open. I crouched down, wrapped her in my arms, and kept saying, "I love you, it's going to be okay." I felt this weight lift off her shoulders. It was as if in that instant, she stepped into a new skin."*

When Kate was a nine-year-old fifth grader she wanted to wear nail polish because my older son, Andy, who is gay, likes to wear nail polish. Andy had long hair and Kate worships the ground he walks on, so she wanted to wear nail polish too. And then she started wanting to wear his shirts to school, which in retrospect were about the length of a dress on her. At the time, I thought this was just her wanting to emulate her brother. She was just different and I didn't know how to pin it down. She wasn't unhappy, but she wasn't happy either. Mostly she was quiet and kept to herself. I asked my son if he thought she was gay and he said, "There's not a gay bone in her body." So when she came out, it was a complete and utter shock. I didn't know what it meant to be transgender. Was that the same as being a drag queen? All I could think was, *Wow, we're on a rocket ship headed to an unknown planet.*

When Kate came out, it was swift and to the point. I had taken her to get a haircut. Her hair was very long for a boy: it was scraggly and down a little past her shoulders. Without being asked, the stylist cut off about five inches, and even then I thought it was too long. But as soon as we left the salon, Kate started flipping her head around like she would when she had all that long hair. And then she burst into tears sobbing, "I can't do anything with my hair, Mom, I can't do anything with my hair." Then, with a sharp intake she said, "You don't get it, Mom-I'm a girl."

We were on Main Street in the busiest part of downtown, and she's standing there crying and my heart dropped like nothing I had experienced before. My whole world just stopped. It cracked open. I didn't know what to do. In that moment it was just me and my daughter, and I could see how much pain she was in. I crouched down and wrapped her in my arms as tightly as I could and kept saying, "I love you and it going to be okay" over and over. In those few seconds, I could feel this weight lift off her shoulders. I'd never had such an experience before, but it was as if, in that moment, she stepped into a new skin. It was instantaneous. Overnight Kate became a different child. She was happy, she wasn't as prickly, and she would skip instead of walk. I was dumbfounded. Here I had a brand new daughter who was relaxed and filled with joy. It was awe-inspiring to experience.

A few days later we were at Target, cutting through the girls' department and she stopped dead in her tracks and said, "Mom, I'll wear this dress if you buy it for me." It was a pink and white short-sleeve sweatshirt dress. My heart seized. And I asked her, "Are you sure you want to wear the dress today?" She was adamant; "I'm going to wear this dress, I really like it." When I lifted it off the rack, Andy shouted :I love you mom—you're buying Michael a dress! So the pink dress came home with us and she wore it to school that Monday.

I worried the whole day, wondering if something bad would happen, if my daughter, who was still going by "Michael," would be ridiculed by her friends and come home crushed. How would her teachers, and the school, for that matter, react to my child who had morphed into a girl overnight? When she finally came home, I asked, "Well, Kate, how did it go?" and she answered "Just so-so. Some kids thought it was weird. But I don't mind. I like my dress." She was nonchalant. My child's conviction that she was a girl and her sense of self were rock solid. There were a couple of kids who got in her face, but she was so self-confident and so very happy that their harassment was like water off a duck's back. She told me, "Mom, they can say mean things to me, but I just don't care." She was amazing. She's just a really tough self-possessed kid, and for the first time I could see she was really at home in her own skin.

Kate went through all of fifth grade being known as *Kate, the boy who wears dresses*. Actually it was *Michael, the boy who wears dresses*, because she didn't change her name until just before the start of sixth grade. We went to court to have her name changed because as she said, "A gal can't be a gal with a name like Michael." When she started the school year, her friends were great. They accepted her new name and enveloped her, as did her teachers.

She still had a tight circle of friends of boys and girls who continued to hang out together and go to each other's birthday parties. We live in Midtown, in a neighborhood I specifically chose when I was looking for a place to live because, with an older gay son, I wanted them to grow up in an accepting environment. I feel really, really fortunate to live where we do.

When we went to court that summer before sixth grade to have Kate's name changed, I was very worried about how the judge would react. She turned out to be extremely understanding.

There were no problems and everything went smoothly. She had Kate come stand with her next to the big bench where she was sitting, read through all her documents with her, and called her by her new name. The judge didn't do this for anybody else on her docket. She said to the whole courtroom, "You've got to listen to this." And then she pounded her gavel and everyone stopped whatever they were doing and looked up. And right then and there, with everyone witnessing, she announced that her name was legally changed to Kate. This little ceremony was more than we hoped for. That judge was just super sweet.

When she started sixth grade with her dresses and her new name and pronouns, the kids didn't have to change clothes for PE, so locker rooms weren't a problem. We were both concerned about the bathroom situation. In the beginning, she would just wait to go and hold it in all day, until she got home. That's a terrible thing for any child to have to deal with. How can anyone learn, doing that? I don't think she was comfortable enough with it then, and I don't think she ever used the girls' restroom that whole year. Today she has no problem using the girls' restrooms in high school.

She endured some harassment, mostly from boys, calling her by her deadname, taunting her as a "fag," telling her "You've got a dick—you're a boy, not a girl." Mean stuff like that. As a parent, you feel awful for your child going through that and you want to protect them. But the truth is, there's not a thing you can do without making the situation worse. Kate just stepped right up and told me, "Mom, you know, people are saying these things at school. But it's okay, I'm handling it. I just blow it off as much as I can. You can't say anything to the school, because if you do, it's just going to get 15 times worse." She was adamant that I not contact anybody at the school.

Kate started puberty blockers when she was in fifth grade and the next year at the end of sixth grade she started hormone therapy. She never went through male puberty; her body developed as a woman's would. She does not have a prominent

Adam's apple or facial hair. Instead she has breasts. She has hips, although you can hardly see them. She's really slender and she's thrilled; though, there is one thing that she can't get over and that's having male genitals. She just can't stand that, and she's wanted to have her penis removed since she was 10 years old. Our agreement is that she'll have surgery before she starts college, which is when I'll have the money to afford it.

While the kids and teachers at school made her transition with relative ease, it was a different story when it came to my friends and family. I lost a lot of my friends when Kate came out. People weren't supportive at all. They told me I shouldn't let her transition. We should stop immediately. I shouldn't buy her girls clothes. That this was just a phase she was going to grow out of, and that I was doing her a great disservice.

I couldn't believe it. I was shocked and hurt because these were people I'd been friends with for years. Privately I was thinking, *You're this shallow? It's not about you, it's not your child. Why can't you support my child? I'm not asking you to change anything. My child is still my child. She's still a human being. She's the same kid that you've seen every day. It's just her gender that's changed. If you loved your child, wouldn't you do the same?*

It's easy enough to say, "Find other friends," but it's really hard to do. I just steered clear of those people who were hostile to Kate's transition or gave me negative feedback or made disparaging remarks about my child. Some of my old friends have come around. It took them forever to stop using her deadname, but I'm back on track with some of them. For some, I don't know if they get it or if it's still too foreign a thing that scares them... like, *Oh no, don't get close to me or my kid's going to turn out trans also!"*

Her biological father, my ex-husband, wasn't with the program either. He was an alcoholic, a cocaine addict, and sex addict—the Triple Crown. I got him in rehab for alcoholism. That's when I found out about the cocaine and the other women.

He spent five months in residential rehab, but quit. That was the end of our relationship. I divorced him when Kate was 14-months-old.

He was furious with me for letting Kate wear girls' clothing. He wanted Kate to join the Boy Scouts and keep on being a boy while Kate wanted to become a Brownie along with all her girlfriends. So my ex was not accepting. He was a macho man who always had to be the king of the show and who always wanted other people's acceptance. Now, all of a sudden, here was something that was out of his control. I think he was embarrassed by her as this macho guy and ashamed to have his "son" come out as a girl. Either way, it was really, really hard for him, and it took a long, long time for him to come around and accept that she was transgender.

He's not a father figure for her at all. He doesn't spend very much time with Kate and he's always dating someone or hanging out with his girlfriends. He picks her up on Tuesdays after school, but she no longer stays at his house every other weekend, like she did until she turned 14 when she could finally say no. He's now just the means to an end. She knows how to push his buttons to get money from him and to have him buy her things. He'll pay for her college education. She's maintaining that connection between them, because she knows that's how she's going to college. But that's the extent of their relationship.

I've really reined back how much my ex-husband was able to see Kate and just did my best to insulate myself from his trash talk. "WHAT DID HE SAY?" I told him that he wasn't allowed to say anything negative to Kate. He could be mad at me all he wanted, but Kate was his child, too. She is his flesh and blood and he has to treat her with respect because she is going to remain his child for a long time.

You would've thought my ex would have been sensitized to difference by his son, Kate's brother Andy, who I realized was more than likely gay by the time he was four-years-old. I had this really strong feeling about it. Andy came out in seventh grade and my ex-husband hit the roof. Andy wore nail polish and a flower crown *and* he went to Boy Scouts. My ex-husband, also named Andy, was so ashamed of Andy, he made him take off his nail polish. He also liked wearing flower crowns. It was very difficult for my ex, because he was living his life vicariously through his son.

My mother was not accepting either. She's deeply religious and said that this path they had chosen was not God's will but Kate's. I told her that Kate didn't choose anything. She was born this way, just like you're born with blue eyes or brown hair. Being transgender wasn't a choice. This was just who she is. It's taken my mom a long time to come around. But she's finally stopped deadnaming her and calls her Kate. When we talk on the phone, she always asks how *Kate* is doing. But I'm still very cautious and I still don't share a lot with her about what's going on Kate's life, just in case.

It's often felt like it was me against the world, which is a lonely place to be. I don't think I would have made it through without the support of my therapist. At first I really mourned the loss of my child. I had a son and now all of a sudden I had a daughter. It was a lot to wrap my head around, even though it was the same person. It shouldn't have made a difference. But it was hard to wrap my head around it. Out of the blue I still feel a sense of loss, wondering what my son would have been like. But my therapist helped normalize the fact that Kate was transgender *and* that it was ok to feel conflicted. She was the one person in my life who supported me when no one else did. She's the one who continues to help me and kept me same throughout this whole journey.

To all those politicians who demonize trans kids for political advantage, I want to tell them, "You're hurting my child. My child has a right to be who she is, regardless of what you think. My child is a person just as much as anybody else's child. And the fact that she's transgender should not matter."

Kate is a great kid and she's hilarious and I love her to death.

I couldn't have asked for a better daughter. I would kill anyone who would try to hurt her and would literally throw myself in front of a bus to protect her.

CHAPTER 6—GEORGIE

PARENT: Georgie
Sexual Orientation: Straight
Gender Identity: Female
Age: 50

CHILD: Kelly
Sexual Orientation: Bi
Gender Identity: Trans Female
Pronouns: She/her
Age: 13

> *"Kelly is autistic, and it's been such a beautiful thing to watch a person become comfortable in their own skin for the first time..."*

Kelly has autism, and autistic kids typically have a lot of sensory processing disorders. Kelly has six. Our pediatrician kept putting me off, saying, "There nothing's wrong with him." I told him that I don't think anything's wrong, either, I just think that something is different and I can't pinpoint what it is.

Finally, two months before he was supposed to start kindergarten, I had a private evaluation by a psychologist. I didn't tell her anything of my suspicions. I told her I just want to see if my child is ready or not for school because I have some concerns. She figured out the autism diagnosis and immediately referred me to an occupational therapist for a sensory evaluation, who found six things. Suddenly the rest of my life made sense.

It turned out Kelly was sensory-avoidant in three areas, and sensory-seeking in three areas. One of the things he couldn't stand is loud noises. And lights. He hated having people put things in his mouth, so he wouldn't let me brush his teeth. This led to a lot of dental work—multiple crowns on a four year-old, which I felt terrible about.

Of the sensory seeking things, the biggest one was that he liked to spin and he never got dizzy. So the psychologist would work with him. He would go to the park, he'd sit on something that spins, get off, get back on it and spin and spin all day. The therapist said that because his vestibular system was under-developed, he couldn't feel or really know his place in space. If he was walking by you or walking by a wall or sitting on a piece of furniture, he would bump hard into you or throw himself down or rub against the walls. Because his brain's spatial perception was underdeveloped, his spatial orientation was off so he didn't know how rough he was being. To this day, he doesn't know how rough he's being. He walks really hard on his heels. If he comes to sit on my lap, he sits down hard. He cuddles our cat a little too aggressively, those types of things.

He likes sensory things on his fingers, so he likes those spinner things. He likes popping bubble wrap. He likes how matte surfaces feel instead of shiny surfaces like on book jackets. He likes velvet, which he describes as really satisfying. I don't know if that calms a spot in his brain. We did a lot of music therapy when he was little with a special set of high-end headphones I bought, and we listened to these horrible songs that stimulated parts of his brain. They sounded like discordant, terrible music that made me want to scream, but they helped him. I bought myself a pair of active noise canceling earphones for when we were traveling recently. He had not experienced active noise canceling before. I had him put on my headphones, turned on the noise canceling, and then his eyes got real big. The airport just shut off. He turned to me and said, "I need some of these, Mom."

Autism is interesting in that it's a spectrum disorder. Everyone experiences autism differently, and everyone's experiences with an autistic person differently as well. I've found with people who have autism—whose intelligence is normal or superior—that they don't know how to read body language, read the room, or social dynamics. If they've been in therapy long enough, they start to get those things, and they start to emote appropriately. Today, after therapy, unless you really know my kid well, I would say you wouldn't think there there's anything going on except that maybe he's a little quirky.

When Kelly was 11, he began asking questions about gender and sexual orientation, telling me he wasn't quite sure how to express it because he didn't have the words. I told him, "Well, there's this thing called gender fluidity where people don't know which gender they identify as. So they go back and forth depending on how they're feeling." I told him that fluidity can look like different things for different people. He decided he was going to be genderfluid for a while, until he figured things out.

Because he has autism he needs concrete steps and explanations for things. He couldn't understand why we have these strict gender roles, why women were told what they should and shouldn't wear. He couldn't understand the double standard. He's an ingenious child, wise beyond his years, but still artless in reading social cues most of us take for granted.

He told me he was feeling uncomfortable with some changes in his body and he felt more comfortable doing less feminine things. He'd requested that we use they/them pronouns and changed his name to Kelly because his deadname began with K. Dad had a hard time with that, but less of a hard time with that than the next phase, which was not only jumping into being Kelly, but also identifying as male.

There are a couple of elements to watching a person become comfortable in their own skin. I think the first one, the most notable one, is the anxiety that exists as nervous energy around that person normally transfers into their relations with others. When that goes away, everything improves. Once he finally figured it out—Oh, I'm a guy, I'm a boy—everything just made sense. It felt like he was trying to fit in before, and now it feels like he's figured it out. So he's calm and content. This is big for anyone's child, but I think it's especially important for an autistic one. And my acceptance of him as a boy has created a new level of comfort and trust in his relationship with me. Things are more peaceful and easy between us. It's a beautiful thing to watch a person become comfortable in their own skin for the first time.

Kelly's dad and I waited a really long time to have kids, because we had a lot of relationship issues. I gave myself until I was 35 to make a decision and then finally at age 36, we had a child and it was the best thing ever for bio-dad. He instantly had a little buddy that he doted on. They played together. Even after we divorced, he would pick up Kelly for fun weekends—climbing trees and going to parks and eating junk food and staying up late together with no routine. Which is not what the therapist recommended for an autistic child who needed structure.

It was after we had a child that I figured out I was the only adult in the house. I have this five-year-old child with a fresh autism diagnosis, I now have to juggle four or five different therapies, I'm doing all the medical appointments, I'm doing all the school stuff, plus I've started working again now that my child has started attending school. My husband not only isn't helping with any of this, but he's acting as if I just sit at home, twiddling my thumbs all day. Even so, I might have been able to deal with that, but I'm not only doing all this alone, I have to deal with him actively pushing against everything I need to do and making it twice as hard to get it done. I ended up in therapy because I hit a wall. I sat on my therapist's couch and said, "I'm crazy. I have to be crazy. None of this makes any sense to me." She said, "You're not crazy; you're just dealing with a lot of crazy things."

A couple of years into this, Dad's carrying so much anger that he almost gets violent with me. He had a rigidly strict religious background. He was raised Baptist, and then he got involved with Pentecostalism in high school; they're even more legalistic. We were married for 21 years and during that time, I grew and evolved like most emotionally immature people in their twenties do. But he stayed exactly the same, just as rigid and inflexible as when we met. I think that's partially due to his own autism.

So he's really struggling with how to reconcile his strict religious morality with the fact that Kelly is his child. Dad has moved to Alabama and he's got a whole new family and Kelly doesn't feel comfortable there. They're all closed minded, and transgender does not compute for them. They tell him, "You can't be transgender, because you had long hair two years ago and you acted like a girl and you were crushing on boys." Blah, blah, blah. You're just confused, or you're just in a phase, or you're doing this because of the autism. So now Kelly prefers me over dad, which is not at all what I wanted.

Dad is also struggling because he realized after six months of this that Kelly has stopped going over there and he's losing his child. Kelly does not want to hang out with him alone under any circumstances. The only way he sees them is if we go together, and I always try to invite someone else to come too, so it kind of spreads it around. He would go over to his dad's, and they would ask him things like, "How come you're not shaving your legs? How come you're not turning into this little girl flirt?" He became really uncomfortable with all of their attention to his appearance. He couldn't understand why his gender, his sexuality, how he looks, his body, were all open for discussion against his consent whenever he was over at his dad's. They made him very uncomfortable, plus they wouldn't let him hide out in his room when he was feeling uncomfortable either. I'd get calls from Kelly at 2:00 in the morning, 4:00 in the morning, crying his eyes out and wanting me to come get him and bring him home. He just hated it.

Unfortunately, one day Kelly heard Dad yelling at me on the phone. Dad thinks therapy is bullshit. Dad thinks transgenderism is bullshit. Dad thinks our kid is just copying other kids and trying to be trendy and blah, blah blah. When Kelly was younger, he used to imitate other people by watching how they were trying to figure out their social dynamics. Now he's almost 14 and dad is saying that Kelly is just imitating other people. No. He's had 10 years of therapy. He knows how to be himself. I've tried to give him words to understand what was happening and to express them. That's it. I don't argue with him. I don't steer him. I try to follow his lead.

Kelly, who heard the whole call, thought, *Wow, my dad thinks I'm bullshit.* So now he doesn't want to go over there at all and he barely tolerates our going to dinner together. Dad misses having one-on-one time with his kid, but I don't know if it's going to happen again. He's terrified and angry and doesn't want to go over there, and I'm not going to make him. I'm not forcing my kid to go over to Alabama where he's mistreated and feels attacked.

To give you a sense of how bad it is over there, Stepmom tells Kelly that I'm committing child abuse by allowing him to bind and that she should report me to Child Protective Services. So whenever he went there, Kelly was afraid they would call CPS on me, try take custody of him, and detransition him.

I've told him, "You don't need to worry about that. I've got all your therapists and doctors and all of my people on my side over here. It's not going to happen. The judges here are a little more forward thinking than the judges in Alabama. Dad would have to file here because that's where we live. Don't worry about this." But I also feel terrible that a 13-year-old has to worry about things like this. Being taken away is not something any child should ever have to worry about. You're dealing with grownups who shouldn't be engaging in this bullshit. It's a hostile environment over there.

They love him, but they don't love who he is. Everything is a moral issue and God is looking down on you and he's very disappointed. God's plan is obviously for a man and a woman to get married and have children. So Dad fully believes he's going to hell. Now he fully believes his child is going to hell, too. In fact, we're all going to hell, so I might as well drive the bus. He does not want God to be angry at his child, who he loves. But he's torn between his upbringing, which says all of this is wrong and his child right there in his face saying, "Love me as I am, Dad. "

An 11-year-old coming out as trans is not a moral issue. There's no question that this is my child and they need my love and support and full acceptance. I can't imagine what it would be like to be a kid that age and feel out of place in my own house, with rejecting parents who are supposed to protect and love me at all costs. At the same time, it's been such an honor to be trusted like that by someone who's old enough to choose whether they trust you or not. And I'm so glad I've been able to be that person for him, because he's certainly got nobody else in his corner at this point.

My mom is also deeply religious. I think my dad is kind of like me, basically an atheist. They live in a very small town. They never leave the house, and their world is very small. They get fed news and information on Facebook, and you know how social media works—it just shows them more and more extreme stuff. So now they're struggling with Kelly's transformation, but not to the extent that we feel uncomfortable being there with them. We don't feel unloved. It's not like that. It's just that my mom honestly thinks I'm going to hell and she's praying for my soul. I feel terrible for her.

For my mom, everything is a moral choice. Including being transgender. And I struggle with that. You can't tell me an 11-year-old is making a moral choice when they're uncomfortable in their own skin. We haven't even told my parents that Kelly thinks he's bi. There's no point. They're not going to know what that means.

Kelly's body started to change early with puberty. At age eight, he was very uncomfortable with those changes. I don't know if some of that physical transition might have triggered the autistic sensory processing stuff, because he has always struggled with transitions, and puberty is certainly a big one. To this day, he still struggles with transitions, like switching activities, waking up early to go do something—anything where he doesn't know the plan or can't control the outcome. He constantly asks me what the plan is. If I say we're going to do something, he wants to know what time and he wants me to commit to everything. I'm pretty spontaneous and he struggles with that. So I've learned how to feed him information in a way that makes him comfortable.

Around nine, when we had the discussion about gender fluidity, he started dressing in a revealingly way and playing around with flirty feminine things and trying to get boys' attention. He wanted me to buy him a bikini bathing suit and it wasn't super revealing but it was a bikini. Then, as he started to grow, it fit him differently. And then he started to want other bathing suits. He started to carry himself a certain way. And he got tall and leggy real quick, with boobs. He started dressing provocatively, posing in the way he would see models and other female role models doing.

I don't know how much he actually understood at that age about what those dynamics meant—as far as puberty and starting to have sexual feelings, and looking at the opposite sex in a certain way—versus him copying his sister, his girlfriends, and MySpace describing his stepsister in Alabama, who is also genderfluid, but not out about it. But when he started to get attention because of doing those behaviors, he started to get really uncomfortable. So it made me wonder: Is he truly being uncomfortable with his gender? Or is this his being uncomfortable with change in general and the attention he's getting?

I also wonder if maybe he had some unwanted negative attention when I wasn't around, someone catcalled him or something. Maybe he had been molested or some creep approached him. At that point, Dad and I were getting divorced and he and I parent and supervise very differently, so I was concerned that something like that went down at Dad's girlfriend's house. I do know his body was regularly a topic of dinner table discussion at Dad's house. Dad's girlfriend also has children. She's an ex-stripper who used to sell sex toys. So I worry that maybe something wrong happened, like he was left unsupervised and someone touched him. I don't know. I don't think we've heard the final word from Kelly on that yet.

Later he asked me for a binder, because he wanted to be flatter. I think he started doing research on gender differences and learned what binders were and wanted to wear one. This was when he started to feel genderfluid. He became uncomfortable with too much femininity. To him, bras were a sign of being feminine and he didn't want that. I don't know that he was all the way expressing male, but he was definitely wanting to be more neutral or more tomboy at that point.

A while after trying genderfluidity, he completely changed. It was like night and day. He got out of the shower one day and came to me and said, "I really hate looking down and seeing this big chest." And he's bigger than I am. He stopped shaving his legs. He was just like, "This is ridiculous." So he moved from his genderfluid stage to trans over about six months. He was going by they/them and Kelly for six months. At the end of sixth grade, he came and said to me, "Mom, I don't feel like I want to be genderfluid. I feel like I'm actually male." I said, "Okay, what does that look like? How do you want to manage this right now?"

He said he wanted to start seventh grade as a boy. So I told him I would see if I could make that happen. I wrote the assistant principal, who was amazing. You can just tell some people were born to work with kids that age. And this guy thrives on it. The kids adore him and he's an excellent mediator.

I said, "This is what's happening and I'm curious how you will manage this and if you have managed this in the past. What about bathrooms? What about locker rooms? What about gendered sports? Will his teachers be allies? Where does this school stand?" He and I had a meeting, and everything was mostly ok, except that Kelly still struggled with our county requiring that he use the bathrooms and locker rooms of his birth gender. But there's a non-gendered bathroom in the health clinic he can use, and there's another non-gendered teacher's bathroom that all students are allowed to use.

The teachers were fine with Kelly. They would still misgender him, because the data in the school's attendance system is still his deadname. The system allows for a nickname, but it doesn't pop up automatically so you have to go to another screen to see it. Now we're looking into the process of changing his name legally. And he doesn't know if he wants Kelly because he's feeling like it's too basic. I told him, "We'll change your name legally once. You've got to find one you'll still like when you're 18."

The reaction of his schoolmates was mixed; I'd say about half and half. There were some who just said, "We're not doing this." They'd make fun of him, saying, "You're really a girl." They'd use his deadname. Asking him invasive questions like, "So what's in your pants?" They're kids, they're mean, they're explicit. Right now, they're all insecure and they're all pecking their way to the top of the pile. But fortunately, so far there's been nothing physical. The new kids who've never met him just look at him and he's Kelly. But he experienced just enough negativity in seventh grade that he has asked to go virtual for eighth.

He's been still very cognizant of the fact that he wants to be with the guys in PE and he's wearing a binder and they're not. Sometimes when they go outside to pee, the guys tear their shirts off and he's really bummed that he can't do that. He's angry that breasts are such a thing in our society and that he can't just go around topless like everybody else and it's not fair.

We have these philosophical debates every day about how much things aren't fair. I try to acknowledge and help him feel all those feelings. At the same time, if he goes too far into how it's not fair and he's miserable, I have to prod him into understanding that, yes, things aren't fair and society has been built upon certain norms and expectations for hundreds of years. We can't change it all overnight. I encourage him to have hope and know that I care and when he's 18, he's going to have a lot more options open to him. But he's also right. There are certain things, certain expectations of men and women, that are just ridiculous. Women can't go topless. Why? Because we have boobs. That's so stupid.

Since Kelly doesn't learn by inference, simply by being around people, I had to learn to break down actions for him. And he would ask me, "Well, why?" I would tell him there's probably not a good reason, that's just the way it is. And then we have these in-depth conversations about culture and politics and rights. It's been and continues to be a fascinating process seeing the world through his eyes.

By age 18, he'll be a full-blown adult and can make all of his own choices free from what I or his dad or anybody else thinks. I'm proactively trying to help him through this transition process. But at the same time, I'm trying hard to do enough of my due diligence to ensure that he's making good decisions and understanding the ramifications of any lifelong decisions.

One day he says to me, just matter-of-factly, "Mom, I need to go to the drugstore. We need to get some stuff." We went down the aisle and he put one of everything in our cart. He wanted to try all of it. So we did that for a couple of years and then we were able to get him on some medication to stop the periods, which was wonderful. It's like birth control—it stops your cycle. The earlier you get on something like that, the less physical development you're going to have. Unfortunately, Kelly didn't get on it early enough to prevent breast development or cramps. Supposedly you can pause puberty, and then if you change your mind, when you stop the medication your body will go back through a normal puberty. I had terrible cycles when I was growing up, so we're both glad he doesn't have to deal with that. Plus he's had a lot of dysphoria around it.

He's seeing a great pediatric doctor here who specializes in adolescent transgender health care, Dr. L. He's wonderful. He had a transgender clinic at the University and now he's with a practice called Queer Med. We haven't had Vitamin T [testosterone] yet, but we're having that discussion . I'm not opposed to him getting on hormones in the next few months. And I'm not opposed to him having top surgery at 16, if that becomes an option.

Dr. L recommended that Kelly see a therapist long enough so the therapist is confident that he understands exactly what he's choosing to do, and that these changes that happen in his body will be permanent, before we do anything. For a couple of weeks now, we've been seeing this therapist, a lesbian from Alabama, who totally gets it. But Kelly has been very frustrated with the time all the due diligence and due process take for him. So I told him, "Show me what you know if you're frustrated. Make me a PowerPoint. Show me your research. I want to know why you think you're mature enough to go on testosterone. And then we can use it as for conversations with your therapist, with Dr. L., maybe even someday with your dad, who knows?"

In just one week, Kelly created this amazing PowerPoint listing the reasons he thinks he's mature enough, the listed different types of research he did for things like hormones, top surgery, and bottom surgery, he reviewed statistics, he found credible sources, and then he wrote his own story. I was so impressed. He's really committed and I wanted him to own it. I'm willing to facilitate it, but I don't want to be perceived as the one driving this, because I don't want to give his dad additional ammunition for opposing it. He already thinks I'm pushing this on Kelly, and that none of this was his idea. He doesn't get that I'm doing this out of love for my child.

Kelly expressed interest in bottom surgery at the beginning, before he started the research. Then he saw some of the statistics on success and how difficult and painful the process can be. I keep telling him that research is being done and it might be a lot better in 10 years. He wants to see what physical changes are caused by testosterone first, because he's heard about bottom growth, and how some people get surgery to change the clitoral hood, to have more exposure.

He's not as obsessed with bottom surgery at this point because, at the beginning, he was like, no one is ever sticking anything inside of me. He wanted it closed up. Now he's thinking maybe we can be kind of flexible there, because it might be kind of fun. Because of this journey, he knows more about sexuality than most kids his age. Physiologically, sexually, he's interested and curious about how everything works, and I keep assuring him that it's normal to be curious and interested, and that it works best when you're in a relationship with someone who cares about you. But these are your choices, I just want you to be safe.

He's going virtual for next year. He had a boyfriend and it was very sweet and cute. He ended up breaking up with them, because they didn't launder their clothes and Kelly couldn't stand the smell. He felt really horrible about it. The kid was also 13. People assigned male at birth maybe don't care about those things quite so much, but then maybe I'm stereotyping. He still has his best friend, Emma. They've been besties since elementary school and Emma's mom, Laura, and I are really close friends. Both kids have autism and Central Auditory Processing disorder, which affects how the brain processes sounds. Kelly and Emma get along great. Laura's a single mom, too, so that's really convenient. Sometimes Laura and I trade off weekends with each other or trade off evenings, so that she can go be with her boyfriend at the nudist resort, or I can go be with my boyfriend at his house. It's interesting that we've been able to find community that way.

Laura raises her kid differently than I do. She's very social and out there and doesn't want her kid sitting around gathering dust in their room and being depressed. So she forces her kid out of the house. Kelly is more like me. He's more of a hermit. He doesn't really care if he leaves the house or not. He likes to get out sometimes, he likes to go for a drive in the car with me. Driving is always the best way to talk to a kid. We go get ice cream and he's got friends. He's very social, well-liked and is well-regarded by his peers. He's very kind.

I think we have successfully gotten to the place where his friends like Emma feel comfortable hanging out at our house, because they know they're completely accepted for who they are. You know how teenagers typically have issues with mom and dad, feeling like they don't understand them. So someone else's parents are always cooler, so we've got a little bit of that vibe going on. But most of the time, Kelly's content to be home and play Xbox and talk with me and hang out with my boyfriend and me.

To other parents with trans kids, I would say, It's not about you. It's not a failure on your part. It's about who your child is. You need to be there for them and support them and love them as they are, not as you think they need to be. This experience has been a struggle in all areas for me. But I also grew in all areas of my life at the same time that this was hitting me. It has not been an easy experience by any means, but it has been a very positive one.

I do think Kelly's dad should be involved in his life. He's his father. But if he's going to harm him emotionally, where is the balance between my kid learning that people aren't always going to be supportive and having difficult people in your life? Especially people who are your parents, who love you. It's complicated. I'm constantly in the middle of that dynamic and it's hard. I don't want to cut his dad off, but if he's going to make Kelly's life painful, I'm definitely going to cut him off and let my kid work that out with him when he's 18. Dad is a flawed human being. He's not capable of being okay with this because he's choosing not to be okay with it. And I don't know how much of that is on him and how much of that is on his upbringing. When you're an adult, you make your own choices and you're accountable. I keep flipping back and forth between being angry at my ex and wanting him to do better, feeling bad that he got hurt the way he did and he's not okay. Life is complicated.

CHAPTER 7—ELIZA

PARENT: Eliza
Gender ID: Female
Sex Orientation: Straight
Age: 55

CHILD: Seth
Gender ID: Trans Male
Pronouns: He/him
Sexual Orientation: Gay
Age: 18

> *"Love and support and gender affirming care enabled my child to blossom. It just breaks my heart that he had to leave the state to do it.*

I had no idea until one day close to Valentine's Day when my kid came home from school in the seventh grade looking dejected.

Hey Mom, my boyfriend broke up with me by note today on the walk home from school.

Oh, honey, I'm sorry. Do you think you'll still be friends? Because you guys were really close?

Yeah, yeah, it'll be awkward, but we'll still be friends. But I'm really surprised he broke up with me because I was going to break up with him because I'm going through some really heavy stuff right now.

Uh, could you tell me about that?

Yeah, sure. Let me go grab a glass of milk… and I'll come back and tell you.

I remember sitting there with a sinking feeling and thinking to myself, really a screaming in my head: *Could you get me a shot of something while you're out there???*

Mom, I've been, I've been dropping some hints.

I'm totally missing them, obviously.

I cut my hair and...

Well, I thought you liked being one of the three girls in school with short hair.

I also told you I never wanted to have biological children.

I didn't want to have kids, and I had you at 37... Are you a lesbian?

No. I'm a boy.

My first answer was the WORST. I said, "Well, that's a completely different kind of sex." And he said, "Mom, it has nothing to do with that." I wished I could've stuffed it back into my mouth. I told him. "I have so many friends who are transgender. But you know me: my gaydar doesn't work well." I'd never thought about it. I have just never been on that plane. And Seth knows that about me. So I don't think he was surprised that I didn't pick up it.

What would any parent do, hit out of the blue with this? You ask yourself all the usual questions: *Is this a stage? Is he watching too much YouTube? Is this really real?* I had no clue. But I went to my transgender friends and asked them a lot of questions. Our town has transgender support organization, and I reached out to them. When our local bookstore hosted an evening for parents with children who were questioning their gender, whether they were trans or nonbinary, I connected with a whole bunch of parents there.

All of those group interactions and conversations really helped me fill in the blanks. But I was still not 100% understanding if this was going to be a real thing for Seth. I was referred to through one of the parents' groups to a local therapist named Ryan, and we met and I shared my concerns with him. He ended up meeting with Seth several times but never really spoke with me. I kept wanting to know what they were talking about, and he told me that when Seth was ready, we'll talk about things. I told Seth I had to tell Dad because I need somebody I can talk to and he told me, "I'm not ready to tell Dad."

I am a former journalist, so I can ask a lot of questions and when I do, I learn about things. I get more informed. Jake, my husband, was a cameraman for a national news station at the time, and he was off covering something. I told Seth. "We need to tell him when he gets home from his trip." So Jake came back in from some hurricane or something, set his camera down on the floor, and Seth told him, "Dad, I have something to tell you." Jake knew immediately it was serious. So he sat on the couch and Seth told him, "Dad, I'm transgender." Jake's response was, "I love you fiercely."

So Jake and I both dove into learning about being transgender. Jake's family fucked him up so bad. He was raised Catholic. Growing up, he didn't know anything about sex, it wasn't talked about. His mom said she should have been a nun, which always sounded wack-a-doodle to me. So he questioned the love of his parents. Jake has always been extremely open with Seth about where babies came from and how they were made. He also wanted his son to know that he loved him no matter what. And that is how we proceeded from day one after Seth came out to us.

Finally, Ryan had all three of us—Seth and Jake and I—in for a visit and it was a good talk. I came out feeing more confident because Ryan was finally helping Seth have some really solid conversations with us.

In one conversation at Ryan's, I told him, "Seth hasn't even had his first kiss yet. I really want him to cream in his pants, have his nipples get hard, and just make sure that this is what he wants to do." I was really hung up on that. Ryan said, "I have been in relationships with all sorts of people of different genders, identities, and sexual orientations, and we've learned to just do what feels good and love each other." Jake and I looked at each other like maybe we have to rethink how we do things in *our* relationship. Maybe we just need to do what feels good, and stop getting so uptight. It helped release all my thinking for me.

I had breast cancer in 2015: I was diagnosed on September 11th and I had cancer surgery on Halloween. My parents and my sister who is a nurse came to live with us while I recovered from my mastectomy and so Jake could keep working and Seth could go to school while I healed. Six weeks after my surgery, my parents went home. And they had only been home for two weeks when my mom called me about having to take an ambulance to the hospital. She was later diagnosed with glioblastoma, an extremely aggressive brain cancer, on Christmas Eve. By Martin Luther King Day, she and my dad had moved back in with us, and ended up staying with us until April. Trump was elected that November, and then my mother died on November 29th.

So 2016 was one big nightmare.

Seth had known he was trans for a long time, but he'd waited until Valentine's Day 2017, when he thought we had our feet under us, to finally tell us. He was only 12, but that's the kind of person Seth is. He knew I couldn't handle one more thing and waited until he felt I was ready, or as ready as one can be.

Since then I've been in groups like SoFFA [*Significant Others Friends, Family, and Allies - Ed.*] and some of the other some parents are just miserable. They are mourning the passing of their daughters and crying the whole time. Well, I certainly am not there. Every time I attend, they hadn't moved an inch forward.

I was so sad for them. I kept talking with them, saying, "I've been able to completely embrace this. Why can't you?" But they just couldn't. I wanted my child to know that I supported him unconditionally. And if he decided to change his mind at some point—which I'm confident he will not, but, if he did—he would know that we still supported him, always.

Georgia starts the school year ridiculously early, in August, so Seth started school in eighth grade as Skye, his deadname. He slogged through the first four weeks being miserable, really miserable, wanting to transition and quit the facade. Most of his friends already knew he was going to transition. He was dressing and behaving more masculine. Then when he came back from Labor Day vacation, he told us, "Let's do it."

I asked him, "Are you sure? Like, Dude, you're going to come back from vacation as Seth." And he said, "Yep, let's do it."

We went to the school and met with the counselor who asked him, "Okay, do you want to stay in chorus? You'll need to move to boys' chorus if you do." Sam said no, and the counselor calmly said: "OK, you're going to have to pick a different extracurricular activity. Well, we'll figure that out. You'll continue with P.E., but there's a bathroom in the gym that is unisex you can use to change. On Fridays, the only day where PE is divided by genders, you'll go with the boys. I'll tell your teachers. Do you want me to come in and handle this? Or do you know how to you do this?" He told her, "I've got it."

And that was it. He did. It was awesome, the way he handled it and then the way the counselor and his teachers responded. He told his friends and immediately started using the boys' bathroom.

Everybody just got it. It made sense, because he was already there and he was so confident in his gender. It was really amazing.

At the end of the school year, I went to talk to the teachers to see if he was ready to go to ninth grade, which is the start of high school. They told me, "He's great, he's ready to go. No problems." Then they asked if they could ask me some questions and I said, "Sure." They wanted to know. "Why did we never see you when Seth transitioned? Why did we never hear one word from you?"

I told them that was his deal. If he needed me, he knew I'd be there. But he never needed me. I asked them, "How was that for you?" And they said—"It was FANTASTIC." They all thought it was great. Well, there you go.

When he came back to school as Seth, they had the first school board meeting that year, and it turned out that Alliance for Defending Freedom, a militant right-wing legal group that had been leading the fight against trans kids, had come to our town. This was some coincidence, since Seth had been the only trans kid coming out at that time.

A lot of adults came together to start a group to counter ADF. It was started at the Methodist Church, because one of the Methodist deacon's children had transitioned, and he knew it was important. It turned out to be this really huge, diverse group of people of all ages, and kids too. We were so fortunate to have them, and SoFFA. The adults and family members would meet separately, Then the kids would meet with trans adults. Both of these were facilitated group discussions. We got a lot of support and guidance.

Our school system superintendent stated that we would uphold Obama's interpretation of Title IX which had recently come out and it allowed students to attend a bathroom of their choice. He put a gay flag transposed over his face on his profile picture on Facebook, and ADF went apeshit. They stirred trouble up in the local newspapers and said they were coming to the September school board meeting and bringing a lawyer to make a case to change the bathroom rules.

It's a four square mile radius, a really small school district. About 250 people in a town of 20,000 came. The community really showed up, and it was a four-hour school board meeting, and everyone who wanted to make a public comment got to say their piece.

I'm a political and a community leader. I started a group called "Stop School Shootings Now." After the 2018 Parkland school shooting we helped lead the national walkout in coordination with the March for Our Lives. I've been deeply involved in politics of all sorts. So as soon as the community found out that Seth was trans, people came to us, "We need you to speak. And if Seth will speak, that would be great, too."

We were like, *Holy shit! We have a decision to make.* Seth and I talked about it: *We either keep it under wraps, which I respect, or we go full out. Because you've got to choose, it's one way or the other.* So we had meeting with Lambda Legal, Southern Center for Human Rights, Human Rights Campaign, *and* Georgia Equality, to learn more about ADF's tactics, what could happen if we spoke out, and basically just prepping us for this school board meeting.

Seth participated in all of it. He decided that he was okay with me speaking but he would speak as well. So we did. There was one particularly vocal family in the community, who ADF were clearly using and then used later to bring another lawsuit. Since we were new to this gig, I said I'd have no problem sitting down and talking with these people before the meeting. And everybody was saying, "Oh, you don't want to do that. That's not a good idea. These people are evil." But the journalist side of me was very interested in seeing who these people were up close and personal. So if they want to meet, then let's do it.

My morbid curiosity is huge, and I was really a newbie. I had no idea the depths to which these people would go. My husband and I sat down and talked with five different deeply religious families who were going to be speaking. The leader of the pack was an African American family whose daughter was at the high school but who had no issue with trans kids using the bathroom. It was completely the parents. The daughter was almost beside the point. In fact, she didn't appear at the meeting, just the parents.

Seth waited in the lobby, ready to be introduced to these people because he was that brave. But they didn't want to meet him. I told these families about our family's challenges: my cancer, my Mom's cancer and death, and that Seth had waited to tell us until he thought we could handle it because he had put our family first, even though he needed and wanted to tell us.

I asked these families: "What would you do? What would you do if this was your child coming to you? I feel we love our children where they are and who they are today. The most important thing is that Seth knows we love and support him now. He may change his mind in the future; but there will never be a question about our love. He knows that he is supported for who he is throughout his life by us, the rest of our family, and the community."

I could see them all tearing up. When they came to the meeting the following day, they all hugged me. Before their comments at the meeting, they met with us and said how deeply affected they were. Even with how it turned out—I don't know—I'll always hold on to that.

But it didn't make any difference whatsoever. We had a victory for a little while. But ADF came back and sued the school system over a kindergartener who was using the bathroom of his choice and they alleged that he sexually abused a girl in there. After all the lawsuits, a DOE investigation found that parents had only heard rumors. But that's what the right does—they panic people with lies and disinformation and then move on. It was all so very sad and unnecessary for the community. And then the family accused moved away, and the woman whose daughter was supposedly abused moved away too. Now neither lives in our district anymore.

There was a documentary-length video done by ADF. It was bad. The people I met with, they are in that video. One woman is still my friend on Facebook, because I like to keep an eye on people and what they're saying. I want her to see me living my values and my truth, and my son being happy. He just started college and he is the happiest boy in the world. It's so great.

We went through a real trial by fire. And I've been in it ever since. Seth has, too. He was so committed during those years, when our trans kids had targets on their backs and that was officially embraced by the administration. If you Google his name, you'll see articles from 2017 until pretty recently. He's a published writer now. The story of what happened—he wrote that up and it was published in his university's journal. He has leaned into activism and it has also propelled him.

In April 2019, I spent weeks at the state capital, fighting our state's abortion "heartbeat" ban. When we lost, we got on a plane that morning and I was just devastated. We flew to San Diego to spend a week with friends and see Southern California. I told Seth I was going to get him fish tacos, take him to see the seals, we were going to walk on the beach, and I'm going to have a margarita. And if we get those things accomplished, it's been a good day, because we're landing early and I'm tired. He said, "Cool." When we got fish tacos, the restaurant bathroom had a sign, *All Genders Welcome.* Sam's eyes got really big, "Mom, look at the sign when you go to the bathroom."

Walking on the beach, we saw a gay male couple holding hands, pushing their baby carriage, and their little kid running out in front of them. And Seth said, "Mom…" And I said, "Yeah, I know. It's awesome."

When we got to our hotel room, the garbage in our wastebasket was separated into two sections, one for landfill and one for recycling. And he's like, "Mom, is this America?" It just hit me so hard that this was like another world for him.

At the end of our trip, we stayed with family friends who had moved to LA. Sam had grown up with the daughter of the family, they were born only months apart. On our last night there, I came into his room to say good night to him, and he was lying in the dark. I climbed into bed beside him to just lie with him for a bit. I realized he was crying. I asked what was wrong, and he sobbed: "I don't want to go home. This is where I belong."

Our friends said Sam could come and live with them, but I said no. "You know where you want to go to college, you're a freshman in high school, you'll be okay. College isn't that far away." He asked about boarding school, but it was $50k a year at the very least, and we just couldn't afford it.

After we were back home for a few weeks, he came down the stairs one day and asked:

"How about a blue state? What if we ask Aunt Becky? Seattle would be good. I could live with her and go to public high school. Or Aunt Amy in Vermont?" I said, "Dude, that is such a big ask." And he said, "Can't we just call?"

So I called Becky and posed the idea. Mind you, she doesn't have kids. She said, "Whoa? Lifestyle change. Let me talk to my Joe." She called back in 10 minutes and said that Joe said, *Of course!* And that was it. So Seth went for his sophomore through his senior year in high school in Seattle, living with Aunt Becky and Uncle Joe.

At first I wasn't going to go help move him in because I thought I needed to be at home, working on politics. But then I reconsidered, I thought, since I only have one kid, I should go. And Seth said, "You're coming? Oh, thanks, Mom. I'm so glad." I suck as a human, but he's just that kind of guy. He was never going to ask too much, but he was so thrilled.

He would phone every day, and we did a lot of FaceTiming. He would call us at 11:00 p.m. when I was falling asleep and say, "I need help with my homework. I'll just read you this paper." We listened. I'm listening with my eyes shut, but I'm thinking, that's really good. I would make a couple of changes, but, Wow. He just blossomed. He was a bad writer when he left Georgia.

I mean, terrible. Mainly because he just agonized over EVERYTHING and seemed to make it worse .But when he got to a high school in a state he liked and started taking dual enrollment college classes in a place where no one gave a shit about his gender, he thrived.

We are also really fortunate to have Queer Med, one of the few clinics specializing in adolescent trans medicine in the Southeast. And the doctor there provides hormones and gender affirming care for kids and adults in I think it's a dozen other states as well. Although that number has probably decreased quite a bit with all of the laws passed against it. I think she moved to the Northeast to live, because of being chased and threatened, but she's still at it, and Queer Med is still open here. In fact, Seth still sees them. He went on testosterone almost immediately after transitioning, and then he had a mastectomy at age 16.

We never saw an endocrinologist because Seth had already started his period, and so we were way past blockers. So I was really happy to have Queer Med to go to because they're just a family practitioner. After meeting with Seth, his doctor told us, "Okay, we'll get you started on testosterone. Here's your script. Go get it."

Seth had asked during that meeting, "Can I still get pregnant if I'm taking testosterone?" My jaw hit the ground. Holy cow. Here's this 12-year-old asking a question I hadn't considered. The doc said, "Yes, absolutely. But you should always have protected sex."

I think testosterone helped him from the get-go. Hormones affected him quite a bit. It did what it was supposed to, but very slowly and gradually, like his voice deepening. I've told him that I didn't think he was suffering from all that much dysphoria. And he told me, "How the hell can you say that? Of course I had severe dysphoria. That's why I'm am transgender, you know." I'm not sure how he processed all of that. I certainly hadn't processed it myself.

He wasn't happy about his body at the beginning of puberty, especially getting a period and growing breasts. But he dealt with it. And it was weird because we always go to a friend's lake house in North Carolina, and he had on a bikini and he definitely had boobs. He didn't seem to have that much dysphoria then. But as soon as he made the transition he definitely had dysphoria and was so relieved to have his mastectomy. He told me, "I definitely want it to be rid of the period. Rid of the boobs." Otherwise he was fine. He didn't want any further surgery because he felt like it wouldn't be worthwhile or helpful.

Today Seth has become someone not to be fucked with. I think that went a long way towards him overcoming all the intolerance he saw from other people. In speaking out as a kid against a national group that had come into our community to take away his rights, he faced organized bullying of a different kind. And he absolutely stood up to it in his community. I believe that's probably one of the reasons he felt so confident moving somewhere else. He had had a full-face visit with the evil that doesn't want him around. That he faced that down, as a kid, is inspiring.

As far as dating, he's on Match or Bumble or some app. And he told me he put FTM in his profile. He's pretty straightforward about things. He's dating a guy who is polyamorous. Seth says he isn't interested in that, but this guy is fun, a good friend and a good kisser. HA! So they're gonna keep hanging out, but it won't go very deep. But he seems really happy and that makes me happy.

What I see from kids today is that they don't care about these things. They don't care about gender. They don't care about sexual orientation. They just do what feels good and they're very accepting overall. His cohort of trans kids is coming of age in a very difficult time. But they have no rose-colored glasses on. Their shit detectors are set on High. They're articulate, and they're smart. And they stand up for themselves and each other.

Our neighborhood has become a little island of blue in a sea of red. I grew up in western North Carolina, which has turned into Trumpland. Madison Cawthorn was the most recent representative and before that was Mark Meadows. So you can imagine what kind of place it is. But I know we have truly impacted their lives. I'm still friends with a lot of kids I went to high school with. So I see them liking posts about Seth being in college and being happy after his transition. And I have people calling me every week to talk about their kids transitioning or questioning or just doing anything they can do to be supportive.

Our kids needs should ALWAYS be between the child, their family, and their health care provider. No one outside of that relationship should be involved. There's no way anybody outside that arrangement can ever understand what's going on. Love and support and gender affirming care have enabled my child to blossom. But it breaks my heart that he had to leave the state to do it. I testified at the state captial before the Senate Committee again, and it was just devastating. I cried and cried. I felt like a failure, *and* I felt murderous. And now I'm questioning why I still live here myself...

CHAPTER 8 – ROCHELLE

PARENT: Rochelle
Sexual Orientation: Straight
Gender Identity: Female
Age: 39

CHILD: Lilly
Gender Identity: Trans Female
Pronouns: She/her
Sexual Orientation: TBD
Age: 12

> *"But she really brought the fire when she testified: "I keep coming back here over and over. Because you keep making me come back here over and over. All I want to do is just to go to school and be with my friends who love and support me, and my teachers who love and support me like any other kid. And your bill is nothing but discrimination." I don't know members were that happy, being yelled at by a 10-year-old. But it was something to see."*

When Lilly she was two or three, I thought, *Oh, you know. She's just spending a lot of time with me, like she wants to wear makeup.* She was never a quote-unquote stereotypical boy. We had toy cars and trucks and little things for babies and toddlers but she never, ever wanted anything to do with that. Which was fine with us. Then, when as she was old enough to express herself, all she wanted was to dress up like her friends. We would

97

go to a girlfriend's house, and she would put on all of their clothes, their bell dresses, and all of that. My husband and my dad both really tried to build her interest in sports and Hot Wheels and other things that they thought they should be doing with their son and grandson. But the harder they pushed, the more Lilly pushed back. Over that year, between like four and five, she really, I mean, she turned every single thing she could into a dress, baby.

Right before she turned four, she said she wanted to walk through Legoland and we went with friend. They have these little kiosks where you can buy just like stuffed animals. And I was like, *No, I'm not spending $30 on this ridiculous stuffed animal from China.* I told her, *When we leave, you can go to the Lego store and pick out anything you want,* because in my mind, the Lego store sold Legos. I was wrong. We went in and they had all kinds of things. So. I was like, *Look at all the zoo sets* or whatever. Remember my husband was still having a really hard time with her gender fluidity. So we turned around, and there was this full pink fairy costume with the wand, the skirt, and the Lego logo on the fairy wings. And Lilly was like, this , *This is what I want. You said I could get anything I want. This is what I want.*

So Kyle was waiting outside with our friends and I was like, *Oh my God, he'll lose his mind.* So I still made her still pick out Legos. But before we're even out of the store, Lilly she was putting on the fairy costume. And the second we walked out the door, this grown man started pointing and laughing at her. And Frank was horrified. And it was the beginning of him insisting that she could only wear that in the privacy of our own house. And so she did. She'd come home from school every single day and put it on. And I was like, whatever. She can go to the coffee shop with me. Nope, he was having none of that.

By the time she turned four, she was refusing to let me cut her hair. I remember the last time she got a haircut. We were actually in Mexico, and she was so unhappy about it. She was not so much telling us, *I don't want to cut my hair.* She just, *I want a ponytail.* My husband was like, "Well, that's not going to work for us." But by the time Lilly turned four, she was like, *Nope, not cutting my hair.*

I didn't feel comfortable forcing my child to cut her hair. It would be a violation of her bodily autonomy. And I'm not going to force one of my kids to do something just because I'm bigger. So that became the first big disagreement my husband and I disagreed on about her girlhood. He was very much— *We're the parents here.* He was raised in a very authoritarian household, and so *we* will tell *her* what she's going to do. And my response was, *Over my dead body. Are we going to forcibly hold down our child to cut her hair? That's insane.*

Every single thing that she could get a hold of she would turn it into a dress, turn it into a hairpiece, turn it into whatever would present as feminine. And by the time she turned five, she had done a pretty good job of presenting herself very femininely despite wearing only boy-clothes in public.

As she got older, she went from this really bubbly, outspoken performer of who would sing and dance, to a kid who just slowly, like, declined. She would work really hard to present herself femininely, even if we'd made her wear all boys clothes, she would still manage to give strangers the impression that she was a girl. If I introduced her to anyone with her birth name, you could watch this wave of confusion come over them. And she's very aware, so after a while, she became totally uncomfortable with going in public. She would ask where we were going and who was going to be there, because she did not want to be around anybody that she didn't know.

My parents and extended family who didn't know what was going on gave her two-year-old sister Cynthia a lot of high femme, stereotypical girl things. Like Elsa jewelry things, which is ridiculous for a two year-old. And Lilly was just beside herself because Cindy got all of the things that she wanted.

So she just hit a wall. She was like, *I can't do this anymore. I can't. I only want girls' presents. I want only girls' clothes. I need Santa to turn me into a girl.*

I told her, "Okay, well, we don't have to wait until next Christmas. I will take you shopping." My husband Kyle and I had a Come-to-Jesus moment. She didn't change her name or pronouns, but we told her," Okay, you can start wearing dresses and skirts to school." She wanted to do the whole: go to a store, pick out clothes, try them in the dressing room, check them out in the mirror—all of that, which I hate doing myself. I told her, "Pick out something and leave. If it doesn't work, we can return it." Nope, she wanted the whole process.

We sent messages to her classmates and their parents, to try to makes sure they knew what was coming. But the kids had already seen her turning every single little rug or mat or napkin into a skirt or long hair for as long as they'd known her. So the response from her classmates was, *Yeah, of course she's wearing dresses. Who cares? Why are you telling us?*

And the parents were farther along than we expected. They were like, I don't know if we've ever had a trans kid but there is no doubt this kid is a girl. When we finally let Lilly wear dresses to school, they were like, *Oh, finally.* About six months later she picked a name that we all agreed on and switched that and her pronouns.

She ended up doing the whole high femme thing—sparkles, bows, and pink—for probably a couple of years. Until she realized, *Oh, I can't ride my bike in this.* And then it sort of like settled back down into more practical attire. And now she, *Fuck y'all and all of your old gender stereotypes*: *if I want to wear a tux, I'll wear a tux.*

With her social transition, there were no policies in place for trans kids, but we never had an issue where the school administration wasn't wanting to do the right thing. They can't ensure that every teacher agrees, but they can ensure that teachers are not doing anything inappropriate with her. Although I'm sure there have been conversations behind closed doors.

This is the very first school year ever that she's had kids talking smack to her. And it is very literally replicated verbiage coming from the right-wing news. I think it's probably a combination of classmates finally being old enough to process her gender. And I think that there is just so much more rhetoric in households around trans issues.

In the March of 2021, I had this moment of realization listening to the debate on the state Senate floor that, *Oh my God, we have spent years educating people, showing them who trans people are, who we are as families, building solid education networks, and all these things are just being completely obliterated in these sweeping five second comments from the right that were nothing but lies.* Legislators have invited the general public into this conversation about whether or not trans kids like my daughter have a right to exist. And that should not be a matter of public debate. But I'm sure it's infiltrated these kids' family conversations more than ever before and that's filtering into what's being directed at Lilly at school.

It was a minority of kids, and there was a concerted effort among teachers and administrators to intervene and educate them. So they're hearing things form school that do not align with what they're hearing at home. And when you're 12, 13, 14, trying to figure out what's real and what's not, it's your parents who have always been your point of truth. And now what they're telling you does not match what you're seeing at school every day.

So they're working these thing through by engaging with Lilly. Her reaction is, *What the fuck? Why would you ever think that's an okay thing to say to me?* It's definitely the hardest thing she's ever had to deal with at school. And we try to be really strategic in making sure that the people who come in contact with all of our kids, not just Lilly, know that their flippant gender bias comments are not going to fly with us.

I see parents and others who think that they're safe because they're in blue states. But I'm watching this slippery slope in blue states where trans kids are getting targeted more and more, because we don't have a concerted effort to counter this insane far right narrative. And they're very coordinated in their efforts.

I have testified several times more than Lilly has.

Lilly testified in the state capital before the legislature for the first time when she was seven, Cynthia testified for the first time in 2021 when she was eight. The thing about going to the capital that people don't realize is that it's really traumatizing for my kids. And now it's getting steadily worse and more hostile. In April, 2021, when Cynthia testified, we had one of our worst days ever. We'd been doing interviews that day for forever and it was just insane. But every time we testify, we far outnumber opposition so my kids get to see tons of people showing up to fight for them. They even have close relationships with legislators at this point, like they're like family. And my kids get to see that they can make change, that they can impact people. So as traumatizing as it can be, it can also be really empowering. And I think it my salvation that to balance all of this insanity they deal with at the Capitol, to find moments of normality and mundane joy for them, with them.

It's outside of our house that we can't control. Our home is a sanctuary for anybody who comes here and we're in this fight together. And she knows that there's a lot of people in this fight with her. I mean, that's part of the being, a part of advocacy and going the capital is that she knows there's a ton of people in her corner. So but she did tell me the other.

We have a ton of people show up for us, and not just in the state capital, but here. We've had city council members there with us. We have people here at the anti-drag protests who are like, *You can take your hate and shove it.* But it's still pretty scary, especially for these kids. I mean, there's videos of adults yelling that they want to kill us. And they've got pictures of us and messages saying they're going to come to our houses. But we couldn't do this advocacy, if we lived in fear all the time.

Before that protest, she knew it was going to happen. I didn't give my kids an option to go because I didn't know how bad it was going to get, having already met with our Police Department and them telling us they were expecting Aryan Nation and Proud Boys.

That was not something I was comfortable bringing my kids to. And just to be clear, it wasn't because drag was happening, it was because of all of these white supremacy extremists. Lilly told me, "I just don't understand why so many people hate me. They don't even know me." And I told her, "Well, these people are just crazy." It's a lot for a kid to take in and deal with.

I mean, it's a pretty fucked up childhood for any kid to have. But the *really* crazy part of I it is, these kinds of things that have been normalized for my children. Having to deal with the hate, having to deal with the legislators, having to show up and defend your right to exist as a trans kid.

Even on the good side, it's still a little nuts. We've gone to Congress, after being invited several times last year. Those kinds of things are just as crazy for any kid to have happen. And it's just been normalized like, *Oh, I've got to go pick up Lilly from school because an LGBTQ advocate from Congress is on the phone and they want to talk to her about how to support trans kids in my state.* That's not normal, it's just kind of bananas.

Lilly's only 12 but she's much more involved in like the advocacy, and legislative process. And we work with Lambda Legal, the ACLU, and HRC regularly. I don't think there's any single national org that we haven't worked with in some capacity. They are all so amazing and doing such crucial work.

I'm not as worried about media. We have a media opportunity, we have a discussion process around it, is this something that is going to be impactful? What is the cost benefit ratio here? It is not about how much media we can get out there. But is this worth our energy? And if it's not, then it's something we don't need to do, because we're also doing advocacy, meeting with legislators, working on messaging, and so many things that are never get to be public facing. Cindy is Lilly's writer, Di, she's here for it too, all of it. So we do it as a family.

Last year, 2021, it all got too hard for Lilly. It was so awful. It was at the legislature in the capital to testify again, and extremists were videoing the kids, and screaming hateful things at them, even inside the hearing room. It was Jeff Younger and his posse of crazy people screaming obscenities at us and calling us "child abusers" and "groomers." It wasn't just us but maybe 10 other parents and kids as well. There were one couple there and the guy started harassing my husband and luckily security stepped in.

We ended up hiding out in the capital, because it was so volatile. We'd been going there for years but we'd never experienced anything like that.

Lilly was just beside herself. She's like, *Mom, I can't do this anymore.* And her little sister Cynthia was like, *Don't worry, I got you.* A couple weeks later, Lily and Cynthia spoke at their first press conference and made 20 or 30 Republican offices visits over three days and. Cynthia picked up where Lilly did not want to participate, and rightly so. It was really, really bad. Lilly didn't even get to testify because the Republicans cut the hearing off. She just sat there crying.

These kids, they show up for each other. They practice their testimonies for each other. Testify together. They practice their office visits on each other and give each other feedback and then go do 18-hour days at the capital together, where they pull up in somebody's office, and then another office, and another. Then they'll go out into the rotunda and practice their power poses or pop into an empty hearing room and sit at one of the desks. By now these kids know their way around the capital like nobody's business.

We've even been harassed at the in the halls of Congress in DC, with the Capitol Police standing right there watching, and not doing anything. That was insane. We couldn't understand why security just stood there watching us get verbally attacked. It was Posie Parker, this TERF from the UK that the Heritage Foundation brought in along with some other TERFS. We were attending this Congressional Roundtable with Trans Equality Task Force with Rep. Joe Kennedy and several other Members of Congress. We had a right to be there and these TERFs

Were waiting for us when we came out and started verbally harassing and pushing us. They went in after State Senator Sarah McBride from Delaware, who is now the highest-ranking trans lawmaker. It was alarming and frightening. And the Capitol Police just stood there and watched. The only bright spot was that Lilly wasn't there for that. Thank goodness it was just adults.

Lilly and Cynthia were pissed when they had to go back to the capital in the fall to testify again, this time against the sports ban. I let them write their own testimonies, and I just sat there sort of stunned when Lilly practiced her testimony for me because she was so quiet. I told her to just make sure that she was loud enough so that they heard her when she spoke.

But oh, no—she really brought the fire when she testified. She told them, "I keep going back here over and over. Because you keep making me come back here over and over. All I want to do is go to school and be with my friends who love and support me, and my teachers who love and support me. And your bill is nothing but discrimination." I was not expecting that. I don't know that members were that happy, being yelled at by a 10-year-old. But it was justified for sure. And it was something to see.

It was such an awful day, knowing that they were going to go in there immediately and pass it out of committee, even though 85% of the testimony was in opposition. They had nothing to stand on.

Just this one person they got up there to testify in support. He was talking about this boy, who would be forced to wrestle with the girls if they don't pass this. He meant Mack Beggs, who was a transboy forced to wrestle girls because he wasn't allowed to wrestle boys. So he didn't even know what he was talking about. He was actually testifying on our behalf, thinking that they were for this bill.

After they ended up passing it out of the house committee, Cynthia was like, *Okay, so are we going to the capital tomorrow to kill it?*

I wished that we were, because the sports bill was the very

105

first bill since we started doing this that made it through. And Cindy is very hard core. She's like, *Well, it's time to go kill a bill.*

Our family has been a mixed bag through all this. I just don't have that much communication with my mom's family anymore. My dad's family has been good though. My family is really conservative. They've turned really Trumpy. But they're not vengeful Republicans, they're not the kind of people who would call CPS on us. In fact, it would be horrifying for my mom's family if we got investigated by CPS.

My grandmother was from Mexico. And the south of the state, where I grew up, is really heavily Latinx, Latino, Hispanic. My husband does not like the term Hispanic: he's Chicano.

We live in a state where everybody seems to have this assumption that we should leave. But we shouldn't have to leave our home. And maybe it's crazy to say so, but we won't. We're lucky because the local DA here has said he won't prosecute families providing gender care to trans children, and the local head of CPS says he won't investigate them. So we have fewer issues in our daily life than many, many families we know in blue states.

It feels like state officials tend to go after parents who attack them too openly on social media, to send a message and scare people off. So while I post a lot about advocacy and activism, I try to be very strategic about what I say and where I post it. In any case, however angry I might be, I've learned to keep it constructive and not attack people by name personally, and adopt a tone that tries to engage rather than attack. Because that's the most effective. .

I think it's really my salvation to balance all of this insanity that we deal with at the Capitol with moments of mundane joy and normality. Just after school, soccer games with friends, hanging out on the weekends. So our kids can also have as normal life as possible for kids who are deeply embedded in this civil rights movement.

CHAPTER 9 – THE PITTS

PARENT 1: Bobby Pitts
PARENT 2: Helen
Sexual Orientation: Straight
Sexual Orientation: Straight
Gender Identity: Male
Gender Identity: Female
Pronouns: He/Him
Pronouns: She/her
Age: 41
Age: 41

CHILD: Tracy
Sexual Orientation: Straight
Gender Identity: Trans Female
Pronouns: She/her
Age: 14

"I tell people, this is something you can come back from. You can come back from anything here and survive. Hey, they got bullied at school. You can survive. Hey, they got caught in the girls' bathroom. You can survive. Go through every other scenario—you can survive. Forty percent of LGBTQ kids consider suicide. You push your kid into that, there's no coming back. So which would you rather have: a trans daughter, or no kid?"

Bobby: I'm in medical sales and she's a hairstylist. Traci has two siblings, one older, one younger. Oldest female. Youngest male. And interestingly enough, the oldest is bi and youngest is gay.

Helen: I would say our eldest definitely leans gay. And I'd say our youngest is probably gay. He's out 100% for sure gay. Tracy said gay and then came out as bi and is now saying she's gay. I'm confused by this part. Before she transitioned definitely gay now as trans woman would technically be considered straight. She thought some women were attractive. So she thought, Maybe that means I'm bi, but speaking of relationships, No, I like boys.

Bobby: I knew definitely that as young as two years old that this wasn't your stereotypical male child…

Helen: Maybe 18 months…

Bobby: We noticed her affinity towards what would be considered feminine toys. She wanted to play with Barbies and dolls and dress up. Not just dress up in dresses, not necessarily. You know, G.I. Joes, fire trucks, race cars and stuff like that. But at that age, well, she's got a big heart at that time. He's got a big sister. So it could be just things that sisters are into.

Helen: All of our kids started walking at about nine or 10 months. She was definitely into stuff. Her sister had a bunch of girly dress up outfits, the heels, the whole nine yards and they're only 24 months apart. She would go and get her sister's dresses out of her room. Not all the time, just it was consistent. Then sometimes she would have a fit when she was three or four to have a dress in the store.

Bobby: There's definitely a period where you think, *Well, your older sibling is always going to be your biggest influence. That's who you look up to.* So we always thought there was a significant amount of imitation or copying—like, I look up to my big sister, I want to do what she does. I went through… I guess you can call it stubbornness, but just falling into the stereotypical, Well, I'm going to get the kids some toys. So I'm going to get a fire truck and a Barbie. I did that up until the age of three, maybe.

Helen: If it was even that long.

Bobby: But there was one Christmas in. We set up all the toys for Tracy in one corner and all the toys for her sister in another corner. And that's the "magic of Christmas," right? Their eyes are supposed to get big, they're supposed to be so happy. *Look at what Santa's brought you!* And Tracy looked at the toys, a fire truck, a police car, all that crap. She just looked at it for like 30 seconds with this major look of disappointment on her face that said, *Why would Santa bring me this crap?* I struggled with this one, but it broke my heart.

Helen: She was only 22 months then.

Bobby: Almost two. And then she immediately walked across the room over to her sister's stuff, which was all dolls and ponies and all this other kind of stuff. I would say, at that point, she was already headed down that path anyway. I thought, *I'm not doing this shit anymore. I don't care. You want a Barbie, you're getting a Barbie. You want a pony, you're getting a pony. I just want my kid to be happy.*

So Helen said, "I've been buying them dolls, right?" So whenever we would go to a Walmart or Target, I would ask her, "What do you want? I don't care." Sometimes she would pick things that are more boyish. Sometimes she'd pick things that our girl would like. I'm not upsetting my kid because of what they're supposed to play with. That was a pivotal, eye-opening moment for us. So this is what she wants.

I'm one of three boys, and 12- and 13-years older than my brothers, so I was an active part of raising them. I'm kind of your stereotypical male. I played football. I played football in college. My dad was in the Army. My brothers are all very much like me, kind of an alpha male. For the most part, I was just doing things I did with my brothers. So, of course, at first, when I found out Helen was pregnant and it was going to be a boy, I assumed he was going to be my football buddy. We're going to do all this stuff.

The whole nature versus nurture thing, I knew pretty quick. No, this is just how my kid is. It wasn't anything we steered one way or the other. It was organic the way she simply grew as our child. Period. You don't know unconditional love until it's staring you in the face. Whatever my preconceived notions of what we were going to do went out the window. Now, that doesn't mean I didn't still try to say, like, *Hey, do you want to watch football with Dad? Do you want to do anything that Dad does just so we could spend time together?* But there wasn't any kind of sense of disappointment—like, Oh no, the kid doesn't want to do this. If my kid doesn't want to do this, they don't have to do it.

Helen: With Tracy, the dress-up stuff was really just primarily dress up, something special. For walking around clothing, she was fine wearing her normal boy clothes. Sometimes she'd pick out a Rapunzel T-shirt or something like that. But for the most part... how do I describe this? It wasn't even really like she was against the male clothes.

Bobby: At that point we were already starting to make assumptions that clearly Tracy is more effeminate, so maybe she will grow up and be gay. That was always my expectation. Well, if a boy is more feminine, they're going to be gay. I hadn't really made that connection yet that they could end up being trans. I think a lot of that is because she was still comfortable wearing boy clothes, and there wasn't any violent pushback against that. I don't think we thought about the trans thing until elementary school in the third grade

Helen: In the second grade, she started wearing more pink and picking out girls' T-shirts. We had those conversations about being aware that not everybody's going to understand why you like that stuff. With things that are outside of societal norms, a lot of people, especially kids, can be judgmental and mean. The mothering part of me just wanted to protect her. I remember in sixth grade, the first time she actually wore a dress to school. Oh my gosh, everybody please be nice. Thinking to myself, Oh my, please have a good day. Please have a good day. But I think she's more resilient than we are.

It's been fascinating to watch her become who she truly is, like her authentic self. You hear about some parents who mourn the loss of their little boy or whatever. I've never felt that. I have the sense of her like any of my children, Oh, you're not my baby anymore, you're a teenager now. Nothing to do with her self-identity or her gender. It's extraordinary that she's been so bold and strong.

I would say for me, probably more in third grade, those years all the close friends were girls, really no strong friendships with boys. If she was invited to a birthday party, it was typically a girl's birthday. I think it was in third grade, probably around that age. We started thinking which direction we're headed far in terms of sexuality.

Bobby: Yeah.

Helen: When she was on swim team or we'd go to our neighborhood pool or pool parties with friends in the community, she didn't want to swim with just swim trunks anymore. She felt naked if she didn't have a swim shirt on. She didn't like exposing her chest, so she swam with little surfer swim shirts or tanks.

Bobby: I was just going to say that we have always tried to be open about it. The most important thing to know is that your family loves you. I remember sometimes Helen would say, "If that's what it is, we'll find out in due time." Maybe we were overdoing a little. Like, *Hey, we're really cool about it.* But Tracy was like, *Don't put yourself in a situation where you have to label me or what I am this point.*

Helen: We always told her that whatever she wanted to wear, we were fine with it. We did tell her it made us nervous. With the whole boy clothing... when she did start wearing more girl or pink stuff we told her that some kids might give her a hard time about that, but that was it. We always told her before she came out as trans that we're fine with whoever she wants to be. You really don't have to check off any boxes if you don't want to or identify one way or the other. We're here to support you. So she identified as a boy for a while.

111

Bobby: Fifth grade was probably pivotal as far as starting to wear women's clothing at home, but not yet at school.

Helen: She got more and more into girl shorts and girl shirts and shoes. But not dresses. Not anything that would scream at you.

Bobby: Of course, here I am trying to try to label and figure out what's going on. *Hey, you know, are you saying maybe you want to be a girl? Because it's okay.* And Tracy was like: *I don't know, Dad. Would you just let it happen when it happens? You'll find out when you find out,* I think our whole concern at the time was just that fear that she was scared to be open with us about who she was, who she felt she needed to be. So we were almost overdoing it saying, *We love you no matter what.* Making sure that whoever she felt she needed to be, we had only that unconditional love.

Helen: There hasn't been a problem with the school or teachers or anything really. But kids can be really mean. Even if it's a straight, cisgender boy who wears pink, sometimes in elementary school he'd get teased. Or his friends get teased for hanging out with him. She was already getting some hard time. All of her best friends were girls and, as you know, she likes to play with the girls' stuff.

Bobby: I think she probably got some teasing and stuff more than she ever let on. I think she had a wall up about that.

Helen: She also got it for hanging out with and playing with girls. She went to girls' birthday parties and did all the girly stuff there. The girls loved her but not all the boys, some of whom are just mean. Kids say what they think and can be cruel and really not even intend to be that way. And whatever they're taught at home. I remember Tracy going to a soccer end-of-the-year party and crossing her legs like a typical female would and some boys taunting, "Why are you sitting like a girl?"

Bobby: Sixth grade is when she definitely started wearing more feminine clothing, though not yet dresses.

Helen: She was trying dresses in sixth grade.

Bobby: I distinctly remember it was January of sixth grade when she came out as gay. *Dad, I like boys.* That was when that officially happened. I was like, *Okay, guess what? That changes nothing.*

Helen: She didn't ever say, *I'm gay.* She just said, *I like boys.*

Bobby: That's sixth grade, well, January of sixth grade in 2020. A few months later, COVID hit. Schools shut down and then going into seventh grade is… No, no, actually, I do remember this. It was seventh grade when they first went back to school. First day of school, she had her outfit picked out. It was a dress. Full blown. There's no mistaking what she's wearing. I remember being terrified that day. I probably checked my phone 77 times day because I was just convinced something bad was going to happen to her.

Helen: That was just this past year.

Bobby: Yeah, that was all female clothing, but not yet, *Hey, I identify as female.* We hadn't officially reached that point that early in seventh grade. I don't think it was until winter break. Maybe because it was over winter break in seventh grade that we had the pediatrician visit. And our pediatrician does a mental health screening with all the patients before they come back. And there are some things that concerned her. And that's when we knew. At that point, at that meeting, that she was potentially interested in transitioning.

Thankfully, when Tracy shared that, with the pediatrician responded with: *The good news is, I've had a couple of patients that have gone this route I don't feel qualified with her age to handle the any kind of hormone prescriptions. But I have patients that have gone down to this practice which focuses on the LGBTQ community.* The doc wanted Tracy to do research and bring her data, then talk. We set up a virtual consultation with one of the provider at the practice, just to have a conversation. But I think more importantly, Tracy put in a lot of homework and had a ton of questions prepared for the providers— *What does transitioning looks like? What is the process? How does it work? What are the results?* I'll never forget when we had that call that Tracy would ask questions and the provider would say, *Yeah, you're going to probably expect this, and then this is going to stop, and then you might have breast development,* and just seeing our kid totally light up and thinking, *Holy shit! This is what we have to do.*

Helen: She was excited about the consultation beforehand. She was so anxious and excited, it was like she was waiting for Christmas to happen.

Bobby: I think she tested the transition waters with friends before parents even though she knew we loved her no matter what. No matter how much you say you love them, there's still fear at having those conversations with mom and dad and how they're going to react? But for us, once it was wearing female clothing, we had already decided this train is headed down the tracks and we know its likely destination.

We were already mentally prepared for where we were headed, but we didn't want to step on the gas pedal to find somebody to get treatments and hormones. We didn't head down that path because we've always been focused on her timeline to guide us. So we're mentally preparing, but we weren't pushing the direction or pushing the progress. It was all at her time and her pace.

Bobby: Nothing bad happened with her schoolmates, or nothing that she shared with us. She came off the bus bouncing like she had the greatest day ever, which for me, was a total relief. I actually got very emotional and had to disappear into the house for a second, because I just had all this pent-up fear the whole day that my kid was going to get the shit kicked out of her. And so to see her get off the bus happy, I had the feeling that, *This might actually be okay.*

I shake my head to think back to our generation going in middle school. There wasn't even an openly gay kid in my middle school. You would have gotten the shit kicked out of you, at least in my house. As a parent, it's always your biggest fear that kids can be cruel. Kids can be brutal. So when she passed that test, I thought, *Okay, maybe this isn't going to be as horrible for my child as I feared it might be.*

Helen: She was already using female pronouns before she told us.

Bobby: I would definitely agree with that.

Helen: It was quite a few months before she said anything to us. I think she tested those waters socially with her friends before she came to us about it.

Bobby: I didn't pick up on it until my oldest kid made a *she* reference. I said, "What do you mean she?" And she was like, "Dad? Oh, okay." It speaks to the optimism I have for this generation. It also speaks to the diversity we have in this area where we live. It's not perfection, but at least it hasn't been what I feared—cruelty, bullying, and perhaps physical confrontations. It hasn't been bad. And she seems to be incredibly popular at school and has a big circle of friends.

At this point, the school hasn't changed her name officially. I think there's a couple of reasons for that. One is that she goes by Tracy among a lot of her friends.. We've asked numerous times, *Do you want to change it official?* But her answer was always, *No, leave me alone. I don't care.* That's very much the teenager side of who she is. She's like, *Whatever. I don't care. Stop asking me.* You just want it to be a social nickname, but not officially on paper at this point? Okay, fine.

A lot of kids, when they change, want everyone to get the pronouns and name and everything absolutely correct. They can be pretty sniffy about that. But it sounds like she really doesn't care. She's comfortable.

Helen: I don't think we got any pushback when Tracy went to "she/her" pronouns either.

Bobby: Yes. To be clear, that part was across the board. No issues whatsoever with that. We didn't get pushback on that at all. In fact, I think they even had a policy in place where you just send an email that said it's done. The only issues we've had with school have been, as you can imagine, bathrooms and locker rooms.

Bobby: The first time I became aware of any issue was in seventh grade when one of the counselors called me to say that she's been using the girls' bathroom. Last year, we made arrangements for her to use one of the staff bathrooms by the clinic up front or by the counselor's office. But she's always been her own advocate. She had a really good relationship with her sixth grade counselor. At that point, even though she hadn't made the transition yet, she already recognized, *I do not feel comfortable in the boys' bathroom.* So she made her own arrangements in sixth grade to use the restroom by the counselor's office. Who knew? She adored her sixth grade counselor.

Then in seventh grade, she just said, *Screw it, I'm not asking for permission.* And she started using the girls' bathroom all the time, usually going with a friend. The counselor would call me to remind us, *We've made arrangements for her to have the gender-neutral bathroom up front, but she's been using the girls' bathroom.* And I'd ask, *Have any students complained about it?* She'd always answer, *No.*

So okay, there's no student issues. So if she keeps using the girls' bathroom for the remainder of the year, will there be any disciplinary action? The counselor tells me, *Well, I don't know if I can say this or not, but no, there won't be.* So I said, *Okay, then nothing's changing.* So Tracy just kept using the girls' bathroom for the remainder of the year. Didn't have any issues. The majority of our trouble came this last year when she registered for PE and she was issued a locker.

Helen: A locker in the girls' locker room.

Bobby: Yeah, in the girls' locker room. About two hours later, a PE coach and a counselor pulled her out of another class to say that, *actually, no, you can't use the locker room. You have to change out in the front of the school.*

Helen: The bathroom they assigned her to use originally was a clinic bathroom.

Bobby: Keep in mind, this is the beginning of 2021. The Delta COVID variant is running wild. We're in a fucking global pandemic. First I'm thinking, *You want my kid to relieve her kidneys in a clinic bathroom where the kids sick with COVID are going?* Then secondly I'm thinking, *Why don't you just put **another** spotlight on this kid?*

We had always let her be the guide of which direction and at what speed we go. It took a couple of days to think about it. *Do you want to stay in and change up front? I can understand if you don't want to, because, Hello? I'm different. I have to change some rules. You don't technically have to change clothes. You want to not change and still do PE?*

Tracy was pretty clear: *I want to either change in the girls' locker like I should or not do PE.* So we dropped PE.

But I told this story to my chapter of *Transparent USA*, and the guy who runs our chapter is a lawyer, and he referred me to the US Office of Civil Rights where I filed a complaint. We found out maybe two months ago that they are going to move forward with an investigation into that.

Bobby: They offered me the chance to do mediation, but I turned it down because I felt like that would give the school an opportunity to just make me satisfied and there's going to be more trans kids going to that school. I told the OCR, "No, we're not doing that. They needed to do it the right way, so I don't know what will come of it." We're off to another school now, but my hope is that they do something.

There's a federal Executive Order that holds, under Title IX, that you can no longer discriminate in schools based on gender identification or sexual orientation. But there're state laws that are different. The US Circuit Court of Appeals has the case. How can a county school board or county school commissioner have more authority than the president of the United States? It was one of those things I don't understand. I don't know how to navigate this world, but it should be easier than this. I didn't know there was any law that said she couldn't play on girls' teams in gym classes. I thought it was just in competitive sports. Interesting

Helen: Well, she can do all the regular gym activities. There's just the lack of being able to use the gym. The gyms at her school are segregated by sex.

Bobby: We're starting at a new high school in the fall. It's one of those things you hate to assume, but I have a feeling they know we're coming. They know we're coming, and I would also say that the high school probably has more experience with gender fluidity than the middle school does. Not as many kids. But I'd be lying if I say I'm not expecting a phone call at some point from the school.

We switched high schools based on Tracy's request. One reason is because she had some friends at the other high school down the street. But the other reason was a valid point when she told us, *Everybody at this high school knows me from pre-transition, knows me physically, as a boy, because the kids from the same elementary school go to the same middle school, then go to that same high school.*

Helen: It's a small high school for our area, only 1,300 kids.

Bobby: I said to her that if you go to this other high school, it's not like we live in New York City. There're going to be kids there who know you're trans. And she said, *Yeah, they might know I'm trans, but they don't know me. They don't know me from before, never seen me from before. So it's kind of a fresh start."* And I said, *Okay, sold.*

When we had the meeting with the counselor there, of course, the first thing was, "Hey, this is the deal…" And she said, "We have a couple of other trans students. Some are not as far along in their process. Some of them aren't even out to their parents. But as far as your girl is concerned, she'll use the girls' locker room and the girls' bathroom. We're here to support her." We both thought, Oh, thank goodness.

I know they've updated everything like her preferred

pronouns. But I don't think the gender marker has been officially updated. I think one of the issues with that in Georgia is you have to have an updated birth certificate and to have an updated birth certificate in this fucking state, you have to have a gender affirming procedure. Obviously, with a 14- not yet 15-year-old, there's not a surgical procedure option for us. So I don't know. It's something we still have to navigate. There's a *Transparent* support group we attend sometimes. Someone there said that they had a doctor write a letter and that was good enough to get their birth certificate changed.

Helen: I don't know. Does a recent passport change that?

Bobby: We did a passport change. So maybe that can help us get it done. But we haven't officially changed the gender marker.

Tracy is also out to my three brothers, and they were cool with it. My Dad was in the Army for 27 years, during the Don't Ask, Don't Tell days. He would admit that he thought a certain way for many years. I can remember when I was in high school, right around the time *Will and Grace* first came on TV and *Ellen* first came out, he told me something like, *Son, if you're gay, I would disown you.* I remember, at that point, not even knowing if being gay was a big thing.

But he was around her enough to pick up on everything. Now, seeing his own flesh and blood, seeing this child with his DNA being raised the same way I was raised, and my brothers were raised, he knows that there's no choice being made here. He said, *It ain't got shit to do with a choice. I was wrong. That's just hoo-hoo. The kid is just being who she* is. So *I got another granddaughter.* And I remember I thought, *Holy shit—that's a great response!*

The day I called him and said, "I just want to let you know we've officially come to that point where she's going to transition. We're going to give her female pronouns, so she's going to be a trans girl." His reaction was, "Well, we've already known. We're just waiting for her to tell us so. Now it's official."

It doesn't happen very often but my wife and I were both out of town at the same time. My mom would usually watch the kids, but she had something going on for work, so the only option we have was Dad. When we got back, he tells me: *I know Tracy usually wears dresses in the house, but not when we go out anywhere. So she came downstairs with a dress on before I took the kids to the movies. And she said, 'Oh, I've got to change real quick.' And I told her, 'Listen, you're going to the movies with your Opa. You wear a damn dress. Nobody's going to mess with you.*

Bobby: Shortly after that consult with the pediatrician she started taking estrogen and progesterone.

Helen: She is also on glutamine, which I guess is like a testosterone type of blocker.

Bobby: It has definitely made an impact. She was at the early stages of puberty, and we knew we had some choices to make. That was one of the things that factored into our supporting going down that path early, is that once puberty kicks in there will be more to change in the future, surgically. I'm a big dude, with very broad, huge shoulders, right? If we go down this path and say, *No, you have to wait.* How do you go back from having a broad shoulders and big arms? You can't suck in your shoulders. But if you start with the hormones, it stops before it even starts.

We noticed pretty quickly her face softening, obviously not turning into a hard jaw line or anything like that, and having some breast development, lack of body hair, things like that. Really the only negative side of this whole thing is she hasn't had the progress that she wants. She wants more and she wants it faster: *I don't want a little bit of breast development. I want lots of breast development, I want it faster*. Things like that. But overall she's been so happy. If I walk in the mall with her right now, nobody would have a clue. That's great. In fact, she almost signed a modeling contract four months ago.

Helen: We told her to make sure they worked with transgender people. I've heard the "growing stealth" story from a number of people, and part of me is deeply envious. The other part of me says that I have never been a parent of a trans kid and I don't have that experience to look back on. But I want to say this. It's hard to feel proud about something that you're also terrified people will find out or that you're been actively hiding. But I also wonder about the long-term effects of hiding something like this. I know some people who are living stealthy and live in terror that someone's going to tell someone and then everyone knows. Obviously, that's an individual choice.

Bobby: Most of the kids from this middle school are feeding into the same high school, they knew her from elementary school, sixth grade. It's one of those things that's going to be pretty well known, but it's not going to be, *Hey, that's the trans girl.* Even if she wanted to go stealth—like she even talked about going to a different high school where some of her other friends were going—that wasn't going to be an option.

Helen: It's not even so much about stealth. She's just a girl. She's living her authentic self. There's no other thing. It's just her being a girl. It doesn't matter how she was born.

Bobby: I'd say one positive sign is she's got a boyfriend, and that's something I definitely didn't expect. He's 16 and she's 14. When she told us, *I like boys,* I said, "Just so you understand, your dating pool just shrunk, right? That doesn't mean that you're not a good person, an attractive person or somebody worth dating. It's just that your options got limited." Is there a trans girl dating pool, I don't even know if one exists. I have no idea.

In typical dad mode, with my oldest being born female and identifying as female, if anybody breaks her heart, I thought, I'll kill them. Here it's the exact opposite. If Tracy gets her heart broken, that means she had a relationship. It's hard to wrap my head around, but it's true. The opportunity to love is worth the pain. If you're being honest about it, you just hope she has a chance for that pain because it means she's had love in her life. That she's got a boyfriend, we are actually both like, *Wow, this is cool. It's going better than planned.*

121

Helen: They're like star-crossed lovers. They're in different high schools. They've been together on and off, mostly on. I think they took a month or two break, but they've been seeing each other for a year.

Helen: Her age deterred the modeling contract. I've had to put a call blocker online from all the calls coming from modeling agents.

Bobby: It's a pain in the ass. As for top surgery or bottom surgery at some point, I would say the answer to that is an emphatic *Yes*. Based upon what Tracy has said to us, that's definitely the path she wants to down. We've heard from others in TransParents USA that have had children go through this that the period between high school and college is usually the best time. We understand that the recovery is it's not as simple as my getting my knee scoped for football, and that the recovery can be tough. The added maturity probably helps. Your kid at 18 getting surgery, versus at 14 or 15, is better. I think that socially it's a good time to make that next step. I'm not sure she even wants top surgery. She definitely wanted faster breast development, but I'm not sure how much more size she wants.

Helen: My sister has like an A-cup and I was always smaller chested. So genetically speaking, that's what you get. But Tracy is like, *As long as I get two breasts, I'll be happy.* So I wouldn't say she wants sizable breasts. She just wanted them to come faster. She's over six feet and built like my sister, who is six feet and maybe 130 pounds soaking wet.

Bobby: She has been sensitive about her height and my mom always says to her, "Damn it, baby, can you please just give me a couple of your inches? Just give me two."

Helen: I'm 5'10" and I have a sister, who's three years older than me, who's six feet and built just like Tracy—super tall, all legs, skinny. So we have a lot of tall folks and I have a cousin who's a cisgender female who is six four. We got some tall girls on my side.

I think she eats crap, like Nutella and Twinkies and moon

pies, but then won't eat a hamburger for dinner. I'm not worried about it, though. She's got that great metabolism.

Bobby: I think the sleeping and eating is more of the typical teenager on display than anything else. I'd say she's well-adjusted beyond expectations, especially this summer has been a great summer for her. She's got something on every day; it's like: *What's on your social calendar today? Whose house are you going to or who's coming over?* But we always have our eyes open and ears open, because for her, there's always going to be challenges that are unique. And sometimes you come down on her for stuff, that's just normal teen stuff. But then, I don't know what it's like to be trans, right? There are clothes all over her room. And I'm like, *What the fuck? Why can't you pick up your clothes?* And Tracy will tell me, *You don't know what it's like to put on 23, 20 different things and just feel like none of them are right for you.* You know, I can't relate to that.

Bobby: We got a therapist who was referred to us that she loves. That's part of her support team. Mental health is just as important, if not more so than physical health. So even when we're doing good, we still keep these appointments, keep having somebody to talk to besides just mom and dad and friends. That's been very beneficial as well.

Bobby: We have major concerns about living in a conservative southern red state making gender-affirming care illegal. They already tried to pass a bathroom bill and a school sports bill. The last two Januarys bills were presented that thankfully didn't make it through the House that would have made it a felony for a doctor to prescribe hormones or puberty blockers. If that happened it would be no questions asked. Immediately our house would be on the market and we're moving.

Thankfully, I have a career where I can live anywhere in the eastern US, but I'd have to leave behind a lot of my family, which would suck, but I'd do it. The other thing is she's got such a good social support network and such good friends here. Sure, we can move to the bluest state there is. But, who knows, we might move to a neighborhood we think is really nice, but is actually full of MAGA assholes who want to harass my kid. We fear that kind of shit. Where can we go and know we're going to be okay? There's definitely real fear.

Helen: To a parent whose kid comes out as trans, I would say, "It's not your journey. IT's their journey to be on. You have to love your kid. You've got to learn how to accept.

Bobby: I've had this type of a conversation with a few people, colleagues and friends. Maybe it's because I'm a sales guy, I try to speak in a way that will resonate with the person I'm talking to. So my first question is, *Do you love your kid?* Because that's a universality among us all—we love our kids, so start there. At the end of the day, you do what you can to protect them. And part of protecting your kid is supporting them along the way.

Because this is something you can come back from. You can come back from anything here and survive. *Hey, I got bullied a bit at school.* You can survive. *Hey, I got caught in the bathroom with other girls.* You can survive. Go through all the other scenarios. I hit them with the statistics form Trevor Project that 40% of LGBTQ youth consider suicide, and it's much higher for trans kids. So which would you rather have: a trans daughter, or no kid? Because if you push your kid into suicide, there's no coming back. There no coming back from that mistake.

In a study of 200 trans adults, two of them changed their minds. Even studies of thousands of kids show that regret rates are 2% or less. Medically I'm sure there are things you can do to detransition to more of a male figure or a female figure. But you can't pull somebody out of a coffin and say, "All right, let's start over. I'm sorry, we should have done this."

You can't. That's a point of no return. So if you love your kid, you need to be supportive. I think the other thing is, if you have the chance to have a conversation with somebody, ask them, "Are you raising them any differently than how you were raised?" I think back again to how I was raised.

That's how I first started with my son. Let's play with this fire truck, let's play with this ball, let's wrestle around. It's very clear to me that this was not a choice she made. This is how this child was born. So, are you raising the kid any different than how you were raised? No.

Then there's another type of personality where I'll borrow a story from one of my buddies, and this is a little crude, but it's the way it is. Your colleague says, "I don't know, I'm not comfortable with this trans stuff, it's probably just a fad or a stage." And you say, "You're super straight, right?"

"Oh, yeah."

"You never once thought about maybe trying out a little Bi."

"No. No."

"You sure? In high school, you didn't suck a couple of dicks just to give it a go."

"No, of course not."

"Okay, you get it now. You wake up every day wired a certain way. It's the same thing."

If you're being honest with yourself, like typical alpha males, you probably sometimes wish you were bisexual because it opens up your options—now everyone's an opportunity. Be honest with yourself; if you could, you'd be wired Bi because then you're open for anybody. But you're not. You are programmed a certain way. This is what you like, what you're attracted to. Do you break it down within specifically cis females? Do you like brunettes? Do you like blondes? Do you like Hispanic women? Do you like white women? It's that detailed in how you're wired and what makes your brain work. Science is fucking real. Yes, it is.

If I could talk to the legislators in the state capital who are considering these bills, I would tell them: *I've never gone to a mayor to get a colonoscopy. I've never gone to a city councilman to have my appendix taken out. I've never gone to a senator to have my cancer treated. You guys aren't fucking qualified in any way, shape, or form to make decisions about medical care for anybody in this fucking country. Whether you're straight, bi, trans, whatever. Period.* It shouldn't even be up for discussion for you all.

The other thing is, overwhelmingly, the majority of this country is supportive of the LGBTQ community. There's not much public support for these laws, yet they're still fucking trying to pass them. And why are they doing it? Because somebody is giving them money to do it. Just look back at the history of your profession, how our senators and congressmen are remembered for being racists—who were against integrating schools, even basic civil rights (they even filibustered anti-lynching bills), and for not allowing biracial marriage—and how they are remembered in history. Guess what? This is how you're going to be remembered. Your grandkids are going to be repulsed by you.

But I want to be positive. Our experience has been special, maybe that's the best way I could put it, because I'm just so grateful we were able to start this journey for her before the puberty train got way down the track. That first meeting with our doctor, to see Tracy light up when she and the doc talked about what the medications would do for her. She was beaming. We've seen the therapy work and how she's developed into a beautiful young woman who turns heads everywhere she goes, who is confident in her appearance. I'm thinking, *Okay, this is a good thing.*

ABOUT THE AUTHORS

Riki Wilchins has 25 years of writing, advocacy, and research on gender and trans issues. She is a founder of the first national transgender advocacy group, GenderPAC, as well as the direct action group The Transexual Menace [sic]. Riki is the author of seven books on gender theory and politics, and her writing has appeared in popular media outlets *The Village Voice* and *Social Text*, peer review publications such as *The Journal of Research on Adolescence* and *The Journal of Homosexuality*, and also her own recurring blog at Medium.com/@rikiwilchins. She has conducted gender trainings for institutions including the White House, CDC, and the HHS Office on Women's Health. Riki's work has been profiled by *The New York Times*. *TIME* magazine selected Riki among "100 Civic Innovators for the 21st Century." She lives in sunny South Beach with her partner, one daughter, two dogs, and three tennis racquets.

Clare Howell retired as a librarian from the Brooklyn Public Library. She was an original member of the Trans[s]exual Menace in NYC and has edited five books with Riki Wilchins. She lives in Guanajuato, Mexico with the library of books she's been carting around for years and now has time to read, and her cat.

Other Riverdale Avenue Books/Magnus Titles You Might Like

By Riki Wilchins

When Texas Came for Our Kids:
How Evangelical Extremists Launched a War on Trans Youth

TRANS/Gressive:
How Transgender Activists Toon on Gay Rights, Feminism,
the Media and Congress

Burn the Binary

Gender Queer: Voices from Beyond the Sexual Binary

Read My Lips:
Sexual Subversion and the End of Gender

Queer Theory, Gender Theory:
And Instant Primer

* * *

Books from Other Authors Published by Riverdale Avenue Books You Might Like

Hiding in Plain Sight
By Zane Thimmesch-Gill

Finding Masculinity:
Female to Male Transition in Adulthood
Edited by Alexander Walker and Emmett J.P. Lundberg

Outside the XY:
Queer, Black and Brown Masculinity
Edited by Brooklyn Boihood

Queering Sexual Violence:
Radical Voices from Within the Anti-Violence Movement
Edited by Jennifer Patterson

Two Spirits, One Heart:
A Mother, Her Transgender Son and their Journey to Love
and Acceptance
By Marsha and Aiden Aizumi